Smashed Avocado and
the Quarter-Life Crisis

Smashed Avocado and the Quarter-Life Crisis:
A Millennial Survival Guide
by Jacqueline Cripps

www.jacquelinecripps.com

Published by Jacqueline Cripps in 2019

Text copyright © Jacqueline Cripps, 2019

National Library of Australia Cataloguing in Publication Data:

Smashed Avocado and the Quarter-Life Crises: A Millennial Survival Guide / author Jacqueline Cripps 1st Edition (2019)

ISBN 978-0-6485645-0-8
ISBN 978-0-6485645-1-5 (ebook)

Cover design by Anis El Idrissi

Book Formatted by Rasel Khondokar

CONTENTS

PROLOGUE

I'm Too Young to Be Having a Crisis. WTF?!

———————o———————

Headline news: **Up to 86 percent of millennials are affected by a Quarter-Life Crisis.**[1] Yes, you read that correctly. Gone are the days of the forty-something year-old 'midlife crisis' that we'd so carelessly laugh about. This crisis is now appearing some 20 years earlier and is biting millennials in the arse at rapid rates. A crisis that probably most of you didn't even know was happening—or had happened—until now.

---

[1] Research undertaken by Dr Oliver Robinson of the University of Greenwich and FirstDirect Bank, indicates 60 percent of millennials experience a quarter-life crisis. Findings of up to 86 percent are supported by a Gumtree.com survey. Note, the quarter-life crisis typically occurs between the ages of 25 and 35, although tends to peak around age 30.

Defined as *'a crisis that may be experienced in one's twenties, involving anxiety over the direction and quality of one's life'*[2] this juicy life segment is now becoming a common occurrence in the lives of millennials.

Don't believe it? Think about the following:

At some point in your twenties—whether now, or in the past—you've tried to complete all the 'right things' for a 'successful' life. A college education at a (probably) private school where you've obtained straight As. A part time job to cover the bills because living out of home is expensive—and relying on your parents doesn't tick the want-to-be-independent box. A university qualification, likely with Honours because of the blood, sweat and tears you put into studying. A job which has the potential to turn into a fantastic career—maybe even for a high paying global company. A relationship—marriage material perhaps, but stable at the very least. Maybe even contemplated kids. In some cases, you may own a home—having survived the 2008 Global Financial Crisis shit storm. Perhaps you've even dabbled in stocks or

---

[2] Collins English Dictionary., 'Quarterlife Crisis'. *Collins English Dictionary*. HarperCollins Publishers, 2018. https://www.collinsdictionary.com.

shares—because let's face it, no one wants to work forever.

You've ticked the boxes of what you think you need to, to be successful in life. To have a successful life. To others, you easily appear to 'have it all', to have 'figured it out' already. Afterall, on face value you do have a plethora of achievements and accolades that you've squeezed out in a very short space of time. In fact, the achievement list that was once a small piece of pencil marked paper, tucked away in the bottom draw of your bedside table, has now become a full-on Excel spreadsheet: listed into categories, ordered by importance and marked off with dates.

Amazing on face value, isn't it? Look at you go!

But the reality is, you are miserably unhappy. You feel physically, mentally and emotionally exhausted. Not able to sleep. Body feeling like a dead carcass that you've been dragging around for as far back as you can remember. Immune system non-existent having cold after cold. Diet consisting of a mix of sugar, caffeine, carbohydrates and alcohol.

You feel unsatisfied, unfulfilled and anxious. Feelings which you've been carrying since your late teens or early twenties. Feelings of uncertainty about where you are going in life—hiding behind a false mask of assurance. Feelings of pressure that you feel from others around you to have your shit together, to be a responsible adult. Feelings of disconnection with the 'you' that is running your life and the 'you' on the inside. Feelings of fear around a want to change—in fact a need to change—but having no fucking idea how. Feelings of being trapped in a life of obligation to follow a certain path—or quite simply, what you feel you 'should' be doing. Feelings of needing to live a life in accordance with the rest of society's wants—so that you can live the dream, of having a happy, fulfilled and successful ever after.

Sound vaguely familiar? There is no denying that you, or another millennial in your life, has not felt this way.

86 percent. Just saying.

Now, to remove the glare of the spotlight above your head, the real issue we need to be looking at is, the 'why'. Why, is our generation—the generation who appear to 'have it all'—falling apart?

Because we face a unique set of circumstances that are not the same as prior generations. The linear pathway of stability and security that may have worked for our parents, the same pathway that is reinforced to us from the moment of birth, **does not work for millennials.**

Times have changed. We are moving away from linear progression of what was once defined as success, and of happiness. The problem is however, while we're in a position where we want things to be different, we're unsure of how, or if, to move forward. The complexity of this dilemma is enhanced by the fact that some of us **don't even know who we are**.

The reality is, the shift in dynamics of life structure and trajectory, and the accompanying revolt that may come with it, is here to stay. There is no going back to the way things were, once upon a time. This is about the now.

We, as millennials, have a responsibility to get to know who we are. To understand ourselves in the context of society, in the context of other generations and in the context of each other. But more importantly, to embrace our authenticity as millennials and harness our power to bring greater good and purpose to the world.

We are not our grandparents, we are not our parents, and we sure as hell are not our children. We are unique, and the contribution we are making to this world—as individuals and as a collective—is setting a new benchmark for living a life that is purposeful and authentic. **A new way of living that is here to stay.**

So, bring your A Game millennials, because this shit, is about to get real.

#Iam millennial

CHAPTER 1

Eenie, Meenie, Miny, Moe: Handpicked for This Life as a Millennial

———————o———————

Generation: *'all the people of about the same age within a society; a period of about 25 to 30 years in which most humans become adults and have their own children.'* [3] *Unless you're the millennial generation, who have no regard for adulthood and babies - instead more focused on taking selfies, littering the world with arrogant, disrespectful views and throwing life savings away on organic and gluten free food - all from the comfort of their couch, because they're inherently lazy.*

Stereotypes aside (because let's face it, there are plenty out there) being a millennial is more than just a label used to describe the group of people born roughly between 1980 and 2000. Admittedly, while it's easier to have a term

———————————————————

[3] Cambridge Dictionary, 'Generation'. *Cambridge Dictionary*. Cambridge University Press, 2018. https://dictionary.cambridge.org.

that helps with categorising groups of people, it's important to remember that specific traits and qualities are generalizations. I stress the generalization point because if you're anything like me, being labelled or defined based on the actions of a group that you happen to fall in to, based on a measurable such as age, doesn't sit well.

We aren't sheep. We are unique individuals, let's not forget that—and like everything in life, there will always be outliers that don't quite fit with what is considered 'typical' or 'normal' of the group. Think, black sheep. Which is of course, totally acceptable. However, while uniqueness in our individual selves will always exist, we can't ignore the fact that research and human behavioural studies have identified a set of characteristics that can be applied to each generation. It would be much easier to revolt against the millennial label if there wasn't a bunch of stats showing consistency with the two and a half billion of us that exist in the world.[4] Some researchers have taken the generation concept a step further—and perhaps a little over the top—by proposing breaking

---

[4] Demographics provided by Pew Research Centre, U.S. 2018. https://www.pewresearch.org.

generations down into 'old', 'middle' and 'new' cohorts, which isn't effective. Why? Well, if we break down every generation into further categories, the notion of generations would become irrelevant. The world would just consist of people, right? So basically, the concept of generations is useful to help us better understand human behaviour in the context of the world and the specific era people are born in.

Now, of course, variations in the strength or persistence of qualities, behaviour and traits will differ. Why? Well, the reality is, the world is always changing. It's a fact. Think about the pace of change in the world today. Things are changing rapidly—and in much shorter periods of time then in the past. Take for example the growth rate of technology. We have a new gadget released in what feels like every month; making wait times gone by look pitiful in comparison. But not just the release, the quality. Think robotics and AI. Technology which in very recent times, has evolved quicker than humans—or so it feels. So, when looking at the rate of change in any environment, a two-decade period is going to be noticed. Which means that a millennial born in 1980 is likely going to express some behaviour a little differently to that of a millennial born in 1995. It's normal.

So, with that said and done, let's get to the point: what does it mean to be a millennial? Before we start unpacking this question and baring our chests so to speak, it's important to raise a couple of points as food for thought.

There is known issue around the fact that millennials are quite probably, the most misunderstood of generations. This doesn't need to be broadcast to you. We've all heard the stigma, labels and assumptions that other generations have free-handedly thrown our way. Resulting in sighs of pity, head-slamming keyboard frustration or silent-or-not-silent 'Are you fucking serious?' statements over the latest slander or gossip. However, if we look at the reasons as to why there's so much bad press, there is no logical explanation—other than simple assumptions which have been made by predecessor generations through misunderstanding. And sure, while we can get our knickers in a twist over who to blame, or give the finger in response, there is no one to blame, nor should there be. There are no guides on how to understand *any* generation and millennials are no exception.

But it isn't just the rest of the world that doesn't quite understand who millennials are. Alarmingly, some millennials don't understand themselves (and yes, this could be you). The world can be a complicated and complex beast to navigate: mixed messages, pressures, societal expectations and ideals, changes fluctuating with world economy, politics, health, poverty—you name it. A range of dynamic factors all thrown together creating what can feel like a whirlwind of uncertainty and instability. Which might not be an issue if you've got a personal manual for navigating life or un-penetrable armour to survive the storm that will inevitably come hurling your way. But the reality is, most of us don't have these options—and even if so, the short-lived benefits would likely end up turning life into a predictable solo journey of boredom.

So, what we think of as a 'plan B' leads us to questioning our lives: what we've endured, where we are at, where we are going and even who we are. There's no problem with questioning our lives. In fact, active reflection and revaluation of our lives is a healthy practice that should be encouraged. Take it from a millennial who's spent a good chunk of her late twenties in reflection: and not just reflection, but serious 'What the fuck am I doing?' reflection with wine and chocolate acting as strong incentives to keep grounded and committed to the process. But I digress. These reflective times often bring about insight and can help us identify areas of our lives, or parts of ourselves, that may need some attention or fine tuning. Providing us with new pathways for improvement or fulfilment.

However, praises for the reflective process aside, it does have the potential to become problematic. Not from an I'm-becoming-fixated-on-incentives-and-rewards point of view (which is an issue for millennials, but more on that later), but when we find ourselves floating about like a leaf in the wind. Or more diplomatically put, when we feel uncertain and insecure. Not just from what is happening around us, but within us. In simple terms, when we don't know who the hell we are.

But before we get into the reasons as to why we end up in this state of being (no thanks of course to everyone else in our lives throwing in their ten cents worth of advice, which could, for some of us, make a great start for a mortgage down payment), let's think about the reality of those words and whether you are one of the leaves being carried and whisked around in the current winds of time.

Bells ringing? Sound of pennies dropping? 'Oh shit!' moments happening? If not, then allow me to entertain you ever so lightly with a stab in the dark.

Scenario one. You're currently thinking to yourself, 'Come on, don't be a fool, of course I know who I am', with your thoughts directed to what you do for a job, where you live, your family, relationships, friends, hobbies, likes, dislikes . . . you get the drift. Things that we tend to associate with 'us' and our 'personality'— rightly or wrongly so (and another juicy topic we'll discuss later).

Scenario two. You've momentarily paused, allowing what you've read to move through your brain for a split second. You might not be quite sure how you feel, or if it resonates, but the word 'hmm' has come to mind.

Scenario three. No response. Your mind is blank, closed off. You're not able to think for yourself, far 'too gone' from the conditioning of the world around you and you find yourself wondering who on earth recommended this god-awful book that's making you think outside of what you know (Joking. It's a great book, which is why you're still reading it).

The reality is, a large portion of people in the world simply don't know, or don't understand who they are. This knowing isn't a knowing like what your favourite food is, your preference for red or white wine, or rom com versus action movie. That's not you. That's the superficial layer (i.e. crap) that you think is 'you'. The knowing being referred to here, is a deeper understanding and acceptance of the essence of who you are—including your purpose and authenticity.

Why the issue you might ask? Think about it. If we as people, don't know or understand who we are, then how are we going to live a life of meaning or purpose? Or live a life that we want, rather than the life of someone else? We can't. Full stop. So how do we solve the problem? For starters, we need to accept that we are never going to be everyone's cup of tea. Fact. It's not a bad thing, unless you decide to take it personally and create unnecessary stress for the sake of it. My advice? Don't.

Yes, we are misunderstood by some, often many. The reputation that society has tagged millennials with, doesn't do us the least bit of justice. But rather than try to revolutionize the misconceptions on behalf of our entire generation, we can take small steps in re-educating those around us. How?

By accepting and owning who we are as millennials. We need to understand who we are in the context of our generation.

Without understanding the uniqueness that make us millennials who we are – a kickass generation—we run the risk of continuing aimlessly through life. Permanently conflicted between what we feel or want, and the rest of the world's expectations.

So, let's begin.

#Idiosyncratic biatches

To start with, we're idiosyncratic peeps. Not necessarily in the quirky or peculiar sense, more that we have a disposition that is exclusive to us. We don't do the ordinary, we do the different. And the value in this approach to life—one that we should we owning with a bit of pizzazz—is to be applauded. What's more? That fabulously instilled BS detector we have, which we can sniff a mile away. And like a Jacki Chan movie, we cut that shit off when we see it. Thanks, but no thanks.

#Openminded not stupid

Complimenting this, is how open minded we are—which may at times have 'the olds' thinking that we're too laisse fair about life. And no, I'm not referring to our generation taking the concept of rainbow unicorns under our wing. As humorous (and ridiculous) as this is, we're a little deeper than that. Think about conversations you've had with older gens around topics such as gender diversity or gay marriage. Conversations that we support, because we're able to shift our perspective and step out of a box of outdated beliefs and attitudes. Now, I'm not saying that all older gens feel this way, or adopt a conservative mindset to life, but the fact is, our appreciation for diversity and the individuality of the authentic self is perhaps a little more obvious. We're not laisse fair, far from it in fact. We do, give a shit.

#Bringing it like Gumby

We aren't set in our ways or our thoughts; rather we are flexible and open to change. This fabulous fluidity isn't just confined to our thoughts and beliefs, but in the very way we live our life. Creatures of habit no more, we take on the variations and colours that life has to offer. You won't find us sitting on the sidelines with our feet dangling in the water. Instead, we gear up in our wetsuits and jump right in. Thrashing ocean or not, you'll find us out there in the thick of it, taking on life and the world as though on a mission.

#Will the real millennial please stand up?

We speak from the heart, from what we know, and we aren't afraid to offer an opinion when we feel it's warranted. Not from a know-it-all perspective, but from an I-like-to-be-heard point of view. While gravely misunderstood by many generations as being 'disrespectful' or 'rude', we simply operate from a place of authenticity. That's it. We can be tactful with the way we express ourselves: 'I see where you're coming from, but with all due respect look at your president. Trump isn't quite the gender equality pin up boy, is he?' Equally, we know when to stop poking the bear.

And while it may erk the older gens that we have a liberal lets-speak-our-mind way of being, the reality is, we're breaking forward from the outdated keep-the-peace mould which has caused enough problems to carry the world through to the next century. Sure, we've got to remember that not everyone is going to ride the wave of speaking from the heart, but the power we give ourselves is golden.

#Peeps of change

We don't like same same, we like different. We want to see more, know more, do more. We don't need a rocket up our arse to get us moving. No, no, no. We just do; operating from an intuitive, natural, purpose driven place of being. A touch of salt here, a dash of sugar there, we like to sprinkle our millennial dust through the interactions we have all over the world. Planting the seeds of what we want, of what we hope will be a legacy. A legacy of something important, of something impactful. A legacy of change, of impact, of creating a world that's better than we left it.

We are people of change, of the greater good; it's why we seek careers that have meaning, careers that have purpose, careers that won't just change our lives, but that of others. Why? Because we care about social responsibility. We care about our world and we seek to contribute toward others.

#Respect for tech

We respect technology for how it's helped shape out world. Not just because it's made our lives easier - like online shopping, UberEATS or Netflix—but it's revolutionised our way of connecting with the world. With an appetite and thirst for 'all things new', including diversity, we've been able to navigate the system to our advantage. And like pigs in mud, content as shit, we light up each time we connect to the differences of the world: cultures, values, beliefs, you name it. We never grow old of expanding our reach, or our connections with others.

#I want to break free (thank you, Queen)

We are an independent bunch, with a want to control our own lives; albeit societal pressures biting at our ankles like chihuahuas. While we typically don't like being told what to do, this is an area where we do unfortunately slip up. Yes . . . falling into a he-says-she-says conundrum of conflicted wants and needs.

Now, with all that said, like all generations we didn't come out of the womb having been designed by Michelangelo. Yes, we have our issues. Yes, we have our hang ups. But if we were put in this world to be perfect then what would be the point? We'd be bored out of a skull and engaging in far more head-slamming-on-desk moments then right now.

Like all gens, we also have our concerns: money, housing, jobs, debts, avocado plantations drying up . . . but that's what makes us relatable to others. If we didn't have concerns, if we didn't have issues to navigate through, then we'd be better off working out time travel, going back up the pipe and stopping conception. It's life. We need to deal with it. And what this book will do is show you how. Why? Well, if you pay enough attention to the conversations being had amongst our gen, it will become obvious. We are not the 'next Gen' or the 'now Gen'. We are the borderline 'lost Gen'. We are lost because sitting on Santa's knee each year and wishing for something better—a puppy, a new toy, a dream job, a lotto win, a seat to Megan and Will's wedding—is not going to happen, nor make life easier.

The reality is, it's becoming more evident that we are living in an era with either our heads stuck up our arse or wearing blindfolds, because we are failing to not only navigate through life but get a grip on who we are. It's time for you to rip off the facade and understand who you are. Not just what makes you 'you', but what game you're playing in life—or, what pawn you are on the chess board.

As it is now, there are too many millennials out there living a life that isn't a reflection of who they—and between you and me it erks me to tears. So, what do we do about it? There's no point playing victim or crying 'woe is me'. The simple fact is, we need to harden the fuck up and deal with it (said with all due respect). Which is what this book is going to teach you: how to put aside cereal box instructions and handle the shit you're facing, so you can live a life that is authentic. Yes, *authentic*.

Conversation over.

P.S. This book is not a fairy-tale.

P.P.S. There will be no participation award, or trophy given, for reading this book.

CHAPTER 2

Mum, Dad, Really? Where Was the Warning About the Real World?

———————o———————

When it comes to relationships, we are greatly influenced—whether we like it or not—by those closest to us. It's these people in our lives who affect our way of thinking, our self-esteem, and our decisions. Take motivational speaker Jim Rohn, who famously stated: 'You are the average of the five people you spend the most time with'. It's rather provoking when you think about it—and makes for an awkward dinner conversation with friends. However, friends aside, have you ever considered how this same level of influence interplays with your parents?

Helicopter parenting is a well-known phrase out there that we millennials get a rap for. That's right. We get a slap across the head for the way our parents raised us . . . go figure. The issue isn't so much about the quasi mollycoddle environment that we grew up in, but the consequences that it has for us later in life. Consequences that we don't know even exist, until we step into what suddenly becomes the 'real world'.

Let me explain.

We are all born into this world on a clean slate, and while putting the notion of equal playing field aside (simply because it's more of a nice to have, rather than the reality), we are all ear marked with an expectation to understand and navigate this thing called 'life'.

Some could argue it's a rather inconsiderate expectation thrust upon us. A deer-in-headlights situation, where we've all become incompetently blinded by the light. Literally (and without the 1977's Bruce Springsteen track to sing along to). This follows of course, a rather awkward journey out of a vagina (or abdomen—either way, both grotesquely traumatic experiences) face planting into life, with a clear absence of introductory textbook, guide or 'how to' manual. Rather, we get a sharp flick on our toes and a slap on the arse to make sure our vital signs are working. Coupled with the false expectation that being bathed in warm water and wrapped in a fluffy blanket, is the way of the future—and how we'll continue the rest of our lives. And people wonder why we grow up with a complex . . .

While we enter the world in what appears to be a neutral state of being, it's very short lived. Why? Because we start interacting with others, which is a catch 22. While human interaction is necessary for our survival, it sets our childhood path—and subsequent adult journey—in either one of two ways: positive or negative. Now, I'm using the term 'negative' loosely here because while shit happens (so to speak), these are just opportunities for growth. So, in the context of putting our first foot forward, the pathways are either formed by us, or for us. Let me explain.

You may have heard on the occasion how fundamental childhood is in shaping who we are—and not just by your therapist. It's one of those fabulous binding qualities for all humans that doesn't discriminate on class, gender or where you live in the world. It's a constant pattern that repeats itself through every generation. It's not a new concept; in fact, debate over genetics vs environment in our development has been discussed (and argued) for years. The answer from a scientific point of view isn't definitive—likely because of the complex variables in making a claim on any one said theory. Let's face it, when we look at all the theories in the world, the one thing that they all typically have in common is a rebuttable theory that exists around the corner. But I digress.

This 'who we are' is made up of our thoughts, values, beliefs and behaviour—including our personality. What this means is that we are, in some ways, 'destined' to become the product of our parents, environment and society. We become conditioned into certain ways of thinking and being. In simple terms, if you had a shit upbringing, then you're likely harbouring issues. Trust me. Conversely of course, if you grew up in a bubble of 'all good things' with oodles of support, then you're more likely going to turn out 'fine' (if that exists).

Without getting too scientific, let me explain simply. Our brains at this early stage in our life are still rapidly developing. They are immature and malleable. That is, all the pathways and connections that the brain is forming, are in a very vulnerable state. Think of the brain like plastic. This vulnerability (which is often overlooked) places us in a position where whatever we are exposed to can have a significant impact. Good and bad.

These impacts, however, are not always observable. Sometimes we aren't even aware we have been impacted, until something in our life acts as a trigger—and we're faced with a whole bucket of 'stuff' to deal with. Think about it. If you've ever been to see a psychologist or therapist, one of the first questions asked is: 'Tell me about your childhood', or 'Tell me about your parents'. Why? Because of this very issue! Now, it's no fault of our parents of course. The reality is, they likely didn't know. Nor did their parents, or their parents' parent. So, it's not about passing the buck or blaming others for our early experiences—it's simply about creating awareness.

You are who you are, because of the influences and experiences you've had as a child. True story.

Most of us have heard the 'Oh, you're just like your father' or 'You sound just like your mother' comments. And rightly or wrongly so, we either gloat or feel sick at the thought. However, if you remove the layer of innocence and think about what said comments can do to a child—such as validating the need to become their respective mother or father—it changes the ball game completely. That is, it's enough to plant a seed so deep in us, that we don't just feel a need to keep behaving or acting in ways to become our parents, but attach our identity into becoming people, that we are in fact, not.

If you're grimacing at the thought of turning out like your parents, then think about this next layer of complexity. Not only do our parents model behaviour which encourages us to develop certain thoughts, beliefs and perspective (or leads us toward a bias to), but if we are fortunate enough to put on our 'reflection googles', we would find ourselves already having received a rather ingrained level of conditioning and influence. Now, in an ideal world—one where we'd all be operating as fully conscious and 'awakened' individuals, having full awareness over every skerrick of information that passes us by—we'd be quick to point out the more-often-than-not unhelpfulness of this. Making the 'Thanks, but no thanks', statement to Mum and Dad far sooner than the adult epiphany moment.

The issue of course here is not so much the influential aspects so to speak—because let's face it, we're all walking around like sponges, sucking up the societal influences that pummel us in every direction on a daily basis—but, the fact that it opens up a well-lit path to absence of ownership and control over our wants. Not to mention the lack of identity we begin to feel, over who we are.

We've all been part of conversations where we've heard someone ask a child, 'What do you want to be when you grow up?' (assuming the term 'grow up' is a reference for reaching the legal adult age and not a level of maturity). Face value wise, it appears innocent. Underneath however, it's another thing altogether. Think poisonous blue ringed octopus, delicately putting out tentacles to lure innocent prey. It's no different. Of course, no one intends to be 'that person' who places a poor innocent child on a career trajectory 15 years before they've even understood the concept of what 'grow up' or 'career' means. But the reality is, there's often a level of harm caused with this type of question.

Think about the child who wants to be an actor but gets told by their parents that there's no money in acting and needs to get 'a real job'. Of course, no child is going to turn about and reply, 'Yeh Dad, I've thought about the definition of 'real job' and realise it's fundamentally flawed. In fact, it's a term laden with judgment, discrimination and status, that places no value on the creative avenues people want to pursue and adds a perception of class to certain jobs that society has classified as mainstream or normal.' The response is more likely going to be, 'What's a real job, Dad?' Which in turn, is responded to by a soliloquy, about what society's 'hot jobs' are, why the child should 'most definitely and without a doubt' pursue said career, and a personal anecdote acting as the hook, line and sinker finale.

It's all rather alarming when you consider it, right? This fundamentally life changing period of our lives that we fail to give two glances at. Impact that occurs well and truly before we've had a chance to fully understand it has happened.

BS, huh?

However, this isn't a blame game (as we've noted before). In fact, as you've probably guessed, if we become the product of our parents, then our parents are simply a product of their parents, and so the cycle continues for all generations across the lifespan.

In fact, to help explain this from a sociological theory-based perspective, we can look to what's called the

Theory of Generations.[5] This theory explains that the era in which a person is born affects how they view the world, due to the various cultural, social and historical experiences that person has. In addition to this, are our values and belief systems, which are shaped in the first decade of our lives and become the drivers of our behaviour and attitudes. Now, on face value this all seems well and good, however, there is a catch. Once our values are established, typically around the age of ten, we tend to keep hold of these unless we experience a 'significant emotional event'. That being, an event or experience that has enough emotional impact to suddenly make us re-evaluate our values or change our perspective in life. And obviously at that age, our perspective-shifting and self-reflection abilities have not developed.

So, we continue growing, becoming adults, guided by our parents. Parents who have the best intentions for us of course—but can't see the downside of their approach or outside of what they know 'works'. And when you don't know what you don't know, it makes it hard to do

---

[5] Also known as the 'Sociology of Generations' or 'Problem of Generations', this theory was proposed by Karl Mannheim in his 1928 essay, *Das Problem der Generationen*.

differently. So, for us, at this critical period of our life, we are hardened into plaster moulds that have been set for us. That is, unless you realise what is happening before it happens—or are at a point where you've realised it has happened and you're ready to do something about it. Which, when push comes to shove, is often coupled with other skeletons in the closest that have raised their heads at the same time.

Now, coinciding with this influence is what we millennials have experienced more than other generations: hands on parenting (aka helicopter parenting). Why? Parental styles and the family structure have seen many changes through generations. When we consider what our family structure is like in the context of other generations, we can see there's no real reason or rhyme, just change. For example, older generations such as our grandparents (i.e. Traditionalists) value a 'until death do us part' approach, where marriage and family structure are of great importance. Conversely, Generation Xers grew up with baby boomer parents in a world of divorce and working mums.

Now, we could try to infer any number of reasons for the changes we've experienced: our parents over compensating for a lack of attention from their parents or having had less enjoyable childhoods; the world having become a different place, with rises in crime, terrorism and sexual assaults contributing to a need for protection; a legitimate want from our parents to see us succeed in life because they love us so much . . . or, due to the simple fact that it's a different era, and therefore is what it is.

While it's debatable if given the choice, we'd have chosen to have parents that wanted to be involved in our lives to the nth degree, the reality is, most of us have come to live with it. Whether the first born, last born, or only born in the family, the drip-fed-verses-osmosis infiltration (so to speak) of incessant parenting has at some point become the everyday. Having said that however, there will always be exceptions to the rule. That being, those of us who experienced a slightly more 'hands off' approach. Which isn't a big deal unless you're suffering from FOMO—in which case I can assure you that you aren't or haven't. Why? Because you've likely been saved from experiencing the world wrapped in a bubble and developed skills that have allowed you to deal with the real world.

Let me explain.

The downside to all this fluffing about from our parents is that we've become to rely on them for, well, everything. I'm not just talking about the basics, like shelter, food and occasional cash. I'm talking bigger things: university choices, job choices, house choices, partner choices . . . and even how to raise our kids. Yes, it's natural to want to go to our parents for advice or a steer in direction every now and then. But the reality is it's become OTT. Enough so to be opening contentious debates on healthy support vs excessive influence.

Let me give you some examples.

We see parents walking into schools demanding that their child is treated better or putting in a complaint to the Department of Education against their child's teacher on grounds of teaching inadequacy because their child didn't get straight A's. We see parents at kids' sports matches making right fools of themselves. Parents who are seemingly reliving their own childhood inadequacies. Incessantly complaining to other parents or arguing with the coach. Screaming at the sideline, 'Dan, keep your eye on the ball!', 'Sophie! Keep with your player! For goodness sake!' or 'What?! That wasn't out! Get your eyes checked, will ya!!' Comments and behaviour which are enough to mortify anyone, let alone a child on the field.

We see parents interfering in college applications: from approving or disapproving the university choice because, goodness forbid, it's not Harvard or Oxford, to writing the application itself. We see parents interfering in exam results: contacting Heads of Faculty because their child wasn't given a 'fair go' or had been suffering from stress and therefore has every right to re-sit their failed exam. We see parents interfering in job interviews: turning up with their child on the day, not least to wish them luck, but to ensure that if the interviewer has any questions, or needs a reference, they're on standby. We see parents influencing house purchase choices: offering cash to help secure a deposit, but conditional on the fact that the house in question also meets their expectations or is preferably located around the corner (we can't be too far away now, can we). The fact is, our parental involvement list is ridiculously long. More alarmingly, is the level of influence is still occurring—not just for us, but for the younger Gen Z, who may experience a wake-up call even more shocking than for us.

Allowing our parents into our lives like this (not that we've often had a choice), has altered in some parts the dynamics of our relationships. We may have found that 'traditional' or 'typical parenting' has become mentoring instead; that we've become friends with our parents, rather than children of. The benefit of this is that we've likely formed or developed more meaningful relationships with our parents. Think conversations about sex, drinking, toilet habits, health—topics we're going to be more open about and discuss, because we see our parents as equal or 'at level' to us, rather than 'above us'. This doesn't mean we respect them any less; in fact, we may respect them more.

However, while this might be ok inside the family home, it hasn't translated in the most appropriate way to the outside world. While we'll get to discussing workplaces later, the downside of the redefinition of our child-parent relationship is it has also redefined our view on authority. That is, we see older generations as our mates too. So rather than conforming to what was once a hierarchical system of order, or chain of command, we're more likely going to act from a space where we see everyone as equal. While it's not an issue for us, it is for others—especially those that feel we're deliberately trying to cut them off at the knees or show a lack of respect. Forming what can become challenging relationships with others, particularly in the workplace (which you can probably now see in hindsight).

Falling fabulously hand in hand with micromanaging parents is the fact that they've also raised us to believe that we're a special generation of humans; or quite frankly, that our shit doesn't stink. This has of course occurred organically and through what would ordinarily be considered caring and supporting parenting—if it hadn't resulted in us developing complexes over spilt milk. I'm sure you can think of umpteen examples of having spoken to your parents about any number of things you've completed, achieved, done or not done and in response you've received a 'Well done!', gift of acknowledgement or become the guest of honour at a small family party to congratulate whatever it is you've achieved. On face value these are wonderful gestures of love and support but have unfortunately shaped our expectations that this treatment is the norm. Not just from our parents, but from the world.

While it would be easy to write off the 'mother hen' approach as an exclusive feature of our parents, there exists another influential player in our upbringing: our teachers. Most of us likely went to a school where achievements were celebrated, and participation was the 'in thing'. While gold stars were reserved for the high achievers, round smiley faces and 'Keep Up the Good Work' stickers were given to everyone else. Irrespective of whether the sticker was gold or not, the reality was, it was a sticker: a reward, a form of acknowledgement and a pat on the back for effort, arousing feelings of 'Yippee!' and making the world a better place. Fast forward to school sports events: athletics, cross county, swimming carnivals. Events that really got schools pumping. Taunting comments here, sabotaging plans there, even bets on the school playground. Yes, there was pressure and yes, there was a want to win first place. Not just for the esteem and recognition, but the trophy. Over time however, the strive for first prize suddenly became irrelevant for us; the meaning lost. We discovered that we didn't need to win first, second or third place to receive an award—we could simply participate and still receive a token ribbon or certificate. But it got even better. For those who fell into the I-loathe-school-sports-event category where turning up with a 'sick note' was the only guaranteed pass, a participation ribbon was often still given. Yes, that's right: a participation award for doing absolutely nothing.

Is there now, any wonder why, that when we've stepped into the real world, we've experienced feeling the equivalent of a violent beating or ended up in a state of crisis? All because we're no longer being given a slap on the back or a high five for breathing.

We've grown up—and are continuing to grow up—significantly influenced by the world around us. As kids we've grown up in a fairyland, protected in a white cloud that has blinded our senses and vision. Our parents have not just shaped our growth and development in helping with our decisions but making them for us. We have had obstacles removed, including effort in decision making. Which is fantastic if we're living in fantasy land, but this simply does not translate to the real world. We have been raised and bred into a generation of what is becoming a more and more popular term: Snowflake[6]. Now, I loathe labels and this term reeks condescension. But, when you

---

[6] A derogatory term used to imply that a person has an inflated sense of uniqueness, sense of entitlement, is easily offended or overly emotional.

look at us, and the generation behind us, does it not surprise you? Particularly when you start thinking about life and realise: 'You know what? I need to harden the fuck up. Thanks Mum and Dad.'

However rather than dwell on it, it's time to put on your big boots and own it. Ten minutes ago, you may never have even realised that you had become this incredible human being—warts and all—as a result of your upbringing. As a result of the way parents, teachers and society have felt, as a collective, was the best way to raise us. While we are now at a point of understanding better who we are, we do have permission—just for a moment— to gently point the finger back at society and say, 'See, look what you've created'. Momentary blame stick aside, it is important to recognise that our strengths in who we are, are also to be attributed to how we've been raised, and we owe that to our parents. They did bless us with the gift of life, after all.

Millennial Survival Techniques

Yes, we've got parents who are involved in our lives—too involved, in some cases. Yes, we've been moulded into people who may have been different if given choice. Yes, our free will has been limited, or taken from us at times. Yes, we've likely been manipulated and influenced against our will. Yes, we've grown up without having to experience the harshness of the world. Yes, we've been falsely led to believe that everyone will acknowledge our efforts, regardless of how big or small. Yes, we might currently feel pissed off at our parents for how we've been raised and having to defend the criticism of the rest of society at our apparent snowflake abilities.

However, this does not make us any less individual, or hinders our choices and power to create and live the life we want. We must recognise and accept that we, as a generation, have been raised in a world that is, and will continue to be, vastly different from once upon a time. Yes, it's affected us in ways that we weren't aware of, or even realised had, until now. But we are now aware and gifted with the power of knowledge. It's time to take responsibility, let go and move forward—all the wiser. Irrespective of who we've become, or what has happened to bring us to this point, we, as millennials, are united by these experiences. Experiences which do not define who we are but help provide context to our lives and in some cases, answers to questions.

#Mollycoddled and survived

CHAPTER 3

WTF Happened with the World?
Millennial Challenges Re-Defined

Millennials get a lot of bad press. Let's be honest. We've all seen the headlines, blogs and opinion pieces pointing out that we're eating ourselves out of house and home, throwing all our money at artisan coffee makers, avocado toast and life experiences—all at the expense of never being a property owner. We've heard the backlash when we rightly stand up and point out that we probably wouldn't be able to afford it anyway: a statement that has more truth than we want to acknowledge.

Let's face it. Shit happens to all of us in life; however, for millennials, the current level is at somewhat unprecedented amounts then once before. In fact, the challenges that millennials are facing on an everyday basis, challenges which are having an impact on our livelihoods, are huge. Now, this isn't to say other generations didn't experience their own sets of challenges during their earlier adulthood—or will continue to. None of us are living in a world wearing titanium suits where we are immune to influences around us. Some of us may deny it of course—and I say good luck to that. You only need to look at some of the current global leaders to realise that avoiding the ripple effects of tantrums, sandpit behaviour and sheer idiocracy, isn't going to happen—at least not forever. Rightly or wrongly so, we are all affected by the political, social, economic and environmental dimensions of the world.

In the interests of simplicity and time management—because you and I both know that our time is precious and we prefer to get to the point without having to sift through layers of unnecessary crap—I'm going to speak from a need-to-know basis about the current challenges that we're facing in the world of jobs, housing and money. If you want detail then please, go consult with the many experts in the field who are far better equipped to give you the *Encyclopedia Britannica* version, should you feel the need.

While having occurred over a decade ago, the Global Financial Crisis (GFC) of 2008 has been a culprit in the current world climate that we are living in. To understand the gravity, the crisis that hit the world — courtesy of the deregulation of the financial industry in the U.S. — is considered to have been the worst financial crisis since the Great Depression of the 1930s. Big deal huh? And finally, after many of us would reply with a 'No shit' response, we now have reports openly stating that millennials have been the generation hit hardest by the GFC.

Stepping outside of the millennial box for a moment, we can see that many of the direct effects of the crisis remain active concerns. Debt levels across global economies, while declining, are still far above where they were before the crisis. And although unemployment rates across the world have started to decline, these remain incredibly high comparative to post GFC. While understanding the effects of the GFC on our generation is far from complete, there are some truths which are evident. The first one being: the world isn't the same as it was post GFC, nor will it be again, so we need to deal with it.

The recession has caused many of us millennials to pause or defer major adult milestones; that is, big life decisions and investments such as buying a home, getting married and having kids. This has seen a dramatic shift in our generation's 'timeline of events' which ordinarily would have happened in our early twenties. Today, these decisions are more likely to be happening toward our thirties—up to a decade behind our parents. But while the ramifications of postponing marriage and buying a home will eventually fade into memory, the economic crisis has left more permanent scars on us. Like generations before us, we have shaped several social and cultural aspects in the world—which is great. Although, whether we're going to be able to leave our mark on the economy in a permanent way, is debatable. Which brings us to looking at the now and the challenges we are facing.

#When I grow up, I don't want to enter a bust economy, have a crap dead-end job and still be dealing with the consequences of a recession. Can we move on already?

Before we continue to milk the consequences of the GFC for all its worth, we must pay tribute to some other historical factors at play which have also shaped our current reality. We all remember having conversations with our parents about what we want to be when we grow up. Faded memories aside, we end up embarking on a chosen career, unfortunately irrespective of whether it's what we want to do. We've barely formed an identify as an adult, yet here we are having to select the 'one thing' to lock ourselves into for life. Consequences no different from a terrible marriage. The truth is, it's often with subconscious trepidation that we select a profession—however, overridden by the prospect that it will work out for us.

So onwards and upwards we go—but not first having the gruelling task of spending the next three to four years a slave to the student system. Pummelling away like hamsters on a wheel. 'Study. Eat. Sleep. Repeat' becomes the story of our lives, with the only variations being booze, sex and part-time jobs. While madly chipping away at what feels like the greatest battle of all time, not once do we consider that when we leave university, we won't have a job. In fact, the thought doesn't even enter our awareness. Why? Because we're led down a path of no questions and perceived certainly; just like Hansel and Gretel. Now, I must preface that this isn't a blame game tactic or tit for tat tales that place emphasis on solving a Whodunnit mystery. This is simply about observation. This is simply about awareness. This is simply about 'it is, what it is'.

#What happened to the market analysis?

It's unlikely that during our Careers Day in high school or college, we challenged the assumption that what was being offered to us as potential careers, was in fact, legit. And by legit, I mean that the career being sold to us was a love-you-long-time career, and not something pulled out of a cereal box: flimsy, cheap and ready to fall apart after a single use. Respectfully said, universities—while having the best intentions for students—also operate as a business. Money needs to be made, and that money comes from us. So, just like any business, they're not going to cut off their supply of income by opening the door to a flaw in the system; that being, the number of graduates versus the reality of jobs available. Universities and colleges will continue to sell the same degree, continue to feed through student production lines, without any real thought for the post-graduation consequences on us.

#Is it a case of false advertising? Can I sue?

The cold hard fact is that completing a degree or becoming qualified in a field does not guarantee a job. The only thing it will guarantee is a hefty student debt that will continue to hang over our heads for the next decade or two—depending on whether we can actually find a job that provides enough income to pay off the debt, and not simply the interest. Yet another harsh reality we soon find out about: the income we receive post-graduation are poor and certainly don't accommodate for the cost of living, which is on the rise.

#Our employment situation sucks

Now, for those millennials who entered the job market during the worst of the crisis may forever be marked by it. Shout out to those in the graduating class of 2008—who entered a baptism of fire by suddenly seeing how the GFC dramatically reshaped the landscape of employment. While headline figures across the world may show improvements as economies have gained some momentum over the past decade, what is obscured are the issues we still have to face: the market, wages, debt and inequality.

Fact: Employment is much harder to find for millennials than it is for any other age bracket. While wishful thinking would have the reason behind this due to a single probable cause, it isn't. There is no simple answer—rather, multiple factors at play.

#Job scarcity is the new norm

Let's start with the market. The current market reflects a huge discrepancy between the amount of jobs that are available versus the amount of job seekers. Employers are being faced with hundreds of applicants for a single job opening. In a world gone by, this competition would have been considered reflective of interest and a healthy market—not because of sheer desperation to be employed. Which means that millennials aren't getting the jobs we want, even after graduation. We are being forced into applying for jobs far below our qualifications. Whether its college graduates applying for retail or coffee shop jobs, to lawyers and Ph.D. graduates applying for entry-level research jobs, the job market has forced many of us to lower our sights. Which is, quite frankly, very depressing. We are applying for jobs well below the ones we would have been competently competitive for in past years.

Exacerbating the issue is that alternate pathways to employment are no longer guaranteed. In the past, we may have been able to go to a temp agency who were once a reliable way to generate income between jobs. But they aren't the answer they used to be. With so many people out of work and competing for the same income sources—even temporary ones—many qualified job seekers find that the agencies they register with go AWOL, never to be contacted again.

#We're overqualified

To rub salt into our wounds, we've unfortunately shot ourselves in the foot by becoming too qualified. This is making employers a lot pickier about who they hire. Because employers today have a smorgasbord of qualified applicants to choose from, simply meeting the job qualifications isn't nearly enough. Which also means that it's much harder for less perfectly qualified applicants to match up to a job that in previous years might have easily been able to secure. So, while having a double-degree or securing a Ph.D. position may look fantastic on paper, you may still need to consider attaching bells and whistle to the application in order to gain attention.

#Job searching is laborious

There's no glamour in job searching, let's be honest. It's painstaking and long—adding strain not just to millennial job seekers, but to workers in general, who lose jobs without any time to get a new one lined up first. What was once a process that might have been wrapped up in a few months, has now become a potential yearlong venture. The result? Unemployment for us is at all-time high.

#Employers may have one up on us . . . for now

For some of us, employers are playing the game—but from the sidelines, watching as we suffer. With today's climate, employers are likely going to have the upper hand—and in some cases, will act like it. It's not uncommon to hear of stories from millennial job seekers who have had to jump through hoops or perform Houdini magic trips, just to be invited to interview. And that's after getting through an online application that doesn't just take a good half a day, but leaves you feeling naked at having to put every intimate detail about yourself on paper. However, neither of those steps guarantees a potential employer getting back to us with a 'yes' or 'no'. Instead, we're left dangling on a thread, uncertain if we should constantly follow up, hold our breath and wait, or keep sifting through the market. Anxiety levels in the meantime, rising. Like temp agencies, potential employers apparently also get sucked down the Bermuda triangle, never to be heard from again.

#We didn't sign up for this shit

Sadly, the millennial generation is suffering the highest rates of job dissatisfaction. If only getting a job was the answer to our problems, right? Nope. We often find when we do get a job, employers still have it in for us.

No matter how transferable our skills might be, the reality is, employers have plenty of well-trained candidates who already meet certain job qualifications or have already worked in the field. Remember the overqualified conversation? That means that even though we might feel we could excel at the job if just given the chance, employers don't have much of an incentive to take a chance on us. Which leaves us feeling like a child who's dropped their ice-cream: anger tantrum versus emotional breakdown.

In what seems like a complete contradiction however, some companies are expecting people to do more with less. While not quite slave labour, in some cases does open a brand-new pathway to burnout. Think workplace restructure, where companies have laid off staff or implemented recruitment freezes for indefinite periods of times. Or, simply not filling positions when someone leaves. Choices of course, often motivated by cost saving, with consequences later manifesting in other ways. However rather than reducing the workload for others, employers simply expect the remaining employees to cover that work, in addition to their own. Resulting in overworked, disgruntled employees: us.

Oh, and then there's the issue with limited upward career progression. Go figure.

#Please retire already

The ageing population hasn't helped like we might have predicted a decade or so ago. There is a growing share of workers older than fifty-five years,[7] who are not retiring—and it's not because of a want. While money has never grown on trees, it's become a darn side harder to cultivate, especially in a world of stagnant wages and rising costs of living. This clearly compounds the job scarcity issue.

#Technology is biting us in the arse

We might be known for our tech savviness, but unfortunately, it's not doing us any favours. The displacement of jobs has increased, with technology and computerisation a key part of that. With the rise of automation, employers are seeing the benefits to both cost and time, and positions that no longer require human skills, are being abolished.

#Wages are low

While a good news story would have millennials being able to make up the lost ground for deferring 'life decisions' as a result of the economy, it's unfortunately becoming out of reach. Early adulthood is typically the

---

[7] Andor, L. 2012. *Employment trends and policies for older workers in the recession*. European Foundation for the Improvement of Living and Working Conditions.

time when productivity is greatest and pay raises more significant: a period where we've all seemed to have hit the fast forward button and skipped this entire segment. Not by choice of course.

We've all heard the saying 'timing is everything' and in this case, it rings true. Think about it. If we're graduating into an economy where jobs are scarce, unemployment rates are high, and wages are poor, there's a high probably that we'll continue to earn less for the rest of our career.[8] Our learned Economist friends have produced reports which have reflected the fact that the median incomes of households, especially those headed by millennials, fell up to 25 percent between 2007 and 2013, compared with the same age cohort in 2007.[9] We are earning up to a quarter less than a decade ago. It's outrageous! Not just this, but we are having to make our money stretch further because the cost of living hasn't

---

[8] Kahn, L. B. (2010). The long-term labor market consequences of graduating from college in a bad economy. *Labour Economics* 17(2), 303-316.

[9] Federal Reserve Bank. (2017). Changes in U.S. Family Finances from 2013 to 2016: Evidence from the Survey of Consumer Finances. *Federal Reserve Bulletin* 103(3), 1-42.

dropped to compensate. In fact, it's risen—quite significantly.

#Goodbye corporate ladder, hello corner desk

But it gets worse. We're finding ourselves backed into a corner when it comes to career progression. Academic research[10] is staring to draw conclusions about the reality of some of us climbing the career ladder. Mostly the older millennial cohort who've become 'stuck' due to being too 'risk averse' post GFC (do you blame us?) or early jobs not providing the skills we need to move forward. Thanks employers.

So, with the job situation having highlighted what appears to be quite literally, a bad news story, is it any wonder why you're now wondering how you've managed to keep your sanity intact? For those of you who haven't, we'll talk more about that later.

#Debt. Sucking the life out of us

It's probably fair to say that between you and I, we've likely clocked up enough debt combined for a hefty

---

[10] Employee Tenure in 2018. *Economic News Release*. Bureau of Labor Statistics, U.S. Department of Labor. 2018.

mortgage deposit. In fact, in some developing countries, we'd have probably owned a five-star resort by now. The reality of our financial position in the 21st century is not one to be celebrated. In fact, it's pretty darn dire, to say the least.

If you've been through university or college, then you're likely one of the millions of millennials contributing to the economic debt of your country, courtesy of the massive student loan debt you're carrying. Debts that—unless you've come from affluence and can pay upfront, the tens of thousands of dollars in course fees—are needed if we want to further our education. Debts that hold us to account for future decisions and actions. Debts of 'type' that complicate the picture further. More of us are financing our higher education using credit, with each student accumulating, on average, more debt than those in the past. However, when we sign up for college, we don't often think too much about the 'when' we are going to have to pay it back. If you're anything like me, you ticked the box on the form that said, 'Yes, I need HELP',[11]

---

[11] The Higher Education Loan Programme (HELP) is the Australian Government student loan scheme. Different countries provide student loans, though terms vary.

and pushed it out of current thinking, somewhere to the back of the brain because it wasn't a 'need to know now' issue. For those who may have pondered on it, due to lingering anxiety or stress about the figures, you may have simply told yourself that it'll be easy to do once you've graduated into the job you've busted your gut for, because you'll finally be earning a decent wage right? Wrong.

The ripple effects of millennial debt penetrate deep into our lives—and not in a pleasurable way. Despite our generation being the best-educated generation in history, those of us holding significant student loan debt are less likely to hold mortgages and auto loans. This debt is preventing us from achieving what were considered normal milestones in adult life, leaving a lot of us pouting about the good days gone by and a 'why me?' complex.

However, as with most of life's events, there is a silver lining. It might not be obvious to us, but as a result of massive student debt, limited employment opportunities, and stagnant wages, millennials are not just straying from historic patterns, we are challenging the status quo. The result? It's having an adverse effect, or what economists predict as a negative impact on the wider economy.

Admittedly, this might not be the ideal legacy for us to be leaving behind, however we are trying to make the best of a shitty situation.

In comparison to our intergenerational comrades, we're considered a 'cheap generation'—and I'm not referring cheap to raise, but the tight-arse type of cheap who won't invest our hard-earned pennies into materialistic possessions. We are foregoing buying houses and cars, not because we don't want these things, but because our eyes are open to the wider world. Sure, we are prevented in most cases from these 'achievements', but we are acutely aware of the financial constraints we have and doing our best to manage it[12].

This change in our spending habits and deferral from buying big ticket items that typically power an economy, has left a scar. Will it change? Unlikely. This offset of the GFC, has fuelled what is being predicted as a permanent generational shift in spending habits and tastes. Gone are the days when purchases just happen. Having become an incredibly cost-conscious generation, we're more likely to

---

[12] Spending patterns of Millennials and earlier generations in 2016. *The Economics Daily*. Bureau of Labor Statistics, U.S. Department of Labor. 2016.

ask the 'why'. That is, why do I need this item? Why will it be the next best thing since sliced gluten free bread topped with smashed avocado? The reality is, we've become more interested in the value of something, rather than the thing itself. And we are reluctant to spend without a clear expectation of value.

Coupled with this, is the value we place in loyalty to a brand and rewards. We are the 'everyone wins a prize' generation, so it's only natural we want to be earning points or coupons that we can at some later point, get a return on. And when push comes to shove, we realise that to be happy, isn't dependent on having a mortgage, a ten-year car loan or some piece of furniture that will become utterly useless.

While we may have hurt the traditional economy by being a little savvier around our spends, we have however, kicked arse in another area. We have revolutionised the sharing economy—or what is known as collaborative consumption, where we share, ride and borrow collectively. Think co-working spaces, car sharing, couch surfing and crowdfunding. Go us.

We are of course also likely annoying the crap out of our parents because we're saying at home longer than before.

In fact, post GFC, some of us older millennials moved back into the family home—relinquishing our independence and becoming teenagers again. On the plus side however, this trend is shifting, particularly for younger millennials who are stepping into a job market which is marginally better than the past decade.

#Savings. What are they?

It's not just us millennials that are feeling the pinch on the rising cost of living and the multitudes of expense we have. Many people feel that even with full-time work, they simply don't have the income necessary to live the lives they want. Yes, as the TattsLotto slogan reminds us, life could be a dream, if we had more money than we could poke a stick at. But it's not only the possibility of a rich and famous lifestyle we've play with the thought of, it's a life where making ends meet doesn't feel so difficult. Even when it comes to the essentials—like food and rent—people complain that money today just doesn't buy what it should. And as it happens, it isn't paranoia, it's a fact. Prices for daily goods have increased considerably in the past twenty years, above and beyond what can be accounted for by inflation.[13] The culprits being higher prices for oil, gasoline, transportation and rent. Unfortunately, the offset of inflation means wage growth is frozen and interest rates rise. Which of course, keeps us stuck in the mud.

Rolling on from this, is with an inability to save any money, retirement will be impacted. Having a spare few dollars to invest into a superannuation account is much harder to part with than times before. Leaving us with a probable future reality of state pensions, if that. Unfair at all? Well, yes. Especially if you also look at the rising inequality that's occurring between older and younger generations. Inequality that's become one of the most glaring and least remarked-upon forms of inequality— and ironically doesn't make headline news. In most countries across the world, we see how rising home values and booming rents have benefitted older generations, while holding younger generations back. Marvellous.

---

[13] Statistics obtained from the Moore Inflation Predictor©, accessed at: https://www.inflationdata.com

#I'll huff and I'll puff, and I'll blow your house down

The housing crisis is the ticking time bomb at the heart of the many economies: wiping out savings, increasing inequality and reducing the ability of anyone, let alone us millennials, to survive the next recession when it hits.

Low cost housing is disappearing from the market. For decades, housing costs have risen faster than incomes. It's not uncommon for us to be spending more than thirty to 40 percent of our wage on rent. But, if you think the rising cost of rent is the only thing impacting our sense of security, think again. Cities with the greatest increases in housing costs also have the greatest increases in homelessness.[14] Think about the rich cities you've walked through: Melbourne, London, New York. Cities that make a stand on the world stage for being fabulous, but literally have people living on the street. It's an appalling juxtaposition. The 'bad guys' creating this issue, are the bigwig rich folk—think investors and private equity firms—who have an increasing habit of buying up

---

[14] Turfrrey, B. 2010. *The human cost: How the lack of affordable housing impacts on all aspects of life.* Shelter, the National Campaign for Homeless People Limited, U.K.

apartment buildings and kicking out current residents. The result? Displacement. And not just of people, but of businesses and services who are being forced out due to cost, and therefore widening the gap.[15]

#Living in a doll house

'When I grow up, I want to live in a house the size of a shoebox, cramped with other people, and in a suburb that I can barely afford', said no one ever. We've seen the words 'crisis' slapped across headlines in the media, referring to the current state for most of us millennials. We already know fairy tales of home ownership and white picket fences have become dusty. In fact, you'd probably find them sitting in the 'less than $1' bargain book bins outside the local bookstore. Today, these old-fashioned stories have been replaced by a condensed two-page synopsis, the title reading: *May the purse be with you.*

At what point did we enter a day and age where we had to bid for a roof over our head? Yes, that's right. Renting bids are happening. Renting wars, in fact. And not to win

[15] Raymond, E., Duckworth, R., Miller, B., Lucas, M., and Pokharel, S. 2016. Corporate Landlords, Institutional Investors, and Displacement: Eviction Rates in Single Family Rentals. *Community & Economic Development Discussion Paper.* Federal Reserve Bank of Atlanta, U.S.

a luxurious pad where we can bask in the glory of our own company. This is just for something that constitutes a brick-and-mortar set up—with mortar not guaranteed. It's like a holiday gone wrong.

How do I continue to love thee?[16] Poems aside, let me count the ways.

Match box living: It seems that those responsible for advertising vacant rooms on the market have taken an incredible warming to the idiom 'packed like sardines'. It's incredibly disheartening to turn up to an inspection to see the definition of 'room' varying from the toilet, to closet spaces, to the central living room couch. Given our affordability position, we are largely having to settle for rooms that might as well have been in the house that George Orwell built.

Unliveable conditions: Grot, filth, grime, mould, insects. Common features of houses these days, which ironically, don't form part of the advertising pack. Anyone would think we were auditioning for Bear Grylls adventures. No, thank you. Pass.

---

[16] *How Do I Love Thee? (Sonnet 43)* was written by Elizabeth Barrett Browning, who was an English poet of the Victorian era.

Overcrowding: It's generally a given when you consider the size of flats and apartments, but for some unlucky folk, it's not just house sharing, but room sharing that's becoming the new norm. Think about this situation. You're sharing a room that would be a decent size for one person, let alone two. You divide the room in half, one houses the bed, the other the floor. Your side of the room is cluttered because the bed isn't an ideal storage space. Your roommates' side is ordered, items strategically placed in a corner, or along the wall. Now because you both believe in fair play, you take it in turns, on a weekly rota, sharing the bed and floor. While you know it's not ideal—simply horrid, in fact—it's the only way you can both save any money, because inner city living is pricey.

Dishonest landlords: Depending on where you live in the world will dictate whether you, as a tenant, have a right in law to a written tenancy agreement. Thought it was a given? Think again. It wouldn't be an issue if everyone in the world operated with pure intent and held the highest morals and values. Ideal world aside, some landlords are taking advantage of this lack of protection. Which unfortunately means that you, dear millennial, are an ideal candidate—and brings me to the next points.

Last minute eviction: Apparently notice periods and common courtesy are a thing of the past. Ever received a text message from your landlord telling you your flat has been sold and you have a month to find new accommodation? Be prepared.

Illegal renting: We've all heard of the tenants who think they're being clever by sub-letting rooms, donning the old 'landlord hat' and making some extra cash on the side. It pays to check, so don't be a sucker.

Invasion of privacy: Yes. Landlords are installing cameras in homes. It's a grey area according to country — both legally and morally. Some of us may get the courtesy of a heads up in the tenancy agreements, such as: 'cameras are installed to end tenant cleaning disputes.' Others of us may be unlucky enough to stumble across one hiding in the kitchen counter cereal box (or lucky, if perversion floats your boat).

Millennial Survival Techniques

Ok, so it appears we've ended up with the short end of the stick when it comes to . . . well, what seems like our basic survival. There's no bet needed: we *are* facing more stressful conditions in our daily lives than older generations. In fact, I'm surprised we're not hearing chants of 'See ya, wouldn't want to be ya' from our non-millennial friends. But, despite what appears to be a tale of gloom for us, we can—and will—make the most of it.

Gone are the days of traditional milestones and stability. We're now living in a world of uncertainty. Trends are no longer predictable; times are not the same. But, when we shift our perspective and let go of feeling like a victim in this 'harsh, cruel world', we can see in fact, that we are the victor. We have broken a mould, challenged the status quo, shaken up the old and re-defined the norm.

Think of it as 'the new adulthood'. A time where we embrace what's happening—and rather than resist, bitch, or whinge about life, put on our strategic cap and make it work for us. A time where we change our perspective, focus and attitude. What if we said to ourselves, this?

You know what, I think not owning a home is favourable, because it keeps me debt free. Yes, it's important to think about investment for the future, but right now, I want to live a life where I'm not tied down to a forty-year commitment that will sit on my shoulders every day, continuing to weigh me down. Besides, a house is only one type of investment anyway and we all know that property isn't safe. The GFC sure didn't discriminate when it hit, blowing out the housing market and all those people losing millions.

Of course, I've heard that rent is 'dead money' but by the time I get to own a home—that is, finally paying off the mortgage because it's not mine until then—I'll probably only get 15 years out of the house before I too, am dead. And then what happens? Oh of course, someone else will reap the benefits of my blood, sweat and tears. Sure, I think sharing and having inheritance for children or family is a noble thing to do, but when did I suddenly have to live a life tied up in obligations for others and not me? Think about the family drama it will also save. We've all seen hell break loose at funerals, or war erupt over who gets what in the will. If my family know I don't own anything then they won't be waiting for me to fall of the perch and then jump into my grave to take what pennies, I have left. In fact, they'll like me for me, not for what I have.

Look, I know that renting sucks, but the fact is, it just is, what it is. It's the new norm and everyone is doing it. Sure, I'd love to live in my own place—who wouldn't—

but if I want to be enjoying my life, then I kind of need to let go. Ironically, we millennials have more power in the rental crisis than we care to realise. Did you know that in some countries we're driving the apartment market? Not just because some of us like to live in inner-city apartments, with more choice over our lifestyle and careers, but because developers are starting to pick up the trends. Think about it peeps. If we're the 'now generation' and at an age where we've left the nest and looking for places to rent, then those big shot developers mentioned earlier, will at some point, come to us. Why? Because we are the people that will ultimately be their rental clientele. Yes, that's right. Smart developers are in fact, right now, coming to us for advice: customising plans to accommodate a more liveable space in accordance with our preferences. Rather influential of us when you think about it isn't it? We're creating our own reality and shaping the new future, off the back of a housing and rental crisis. Resilient bunch, aren't we?

The cost of living is hard. In fact, it's the biggest pinch and I hate every month when I budget, seeing how much is going out the door and not a drop of savings left. But, it's a global issue and not a direct target at me or the millennial clan. Most people are feeling the impact. However, it's not enough to keep me in a box, or blind sighted from options. There are always options. Sure, I might have to make compromises in where I live, who I live with or how I spend my money, but this isn't going to stop me from living and leading a happy and fulfilling life. Yes, I know, who wouldn't want to eat avocado every day, but those things are starting to get pricey. And we all know that consumerism is built on buyers' trends—so growers should be thanking us millennials for putting avocados on the world stage and making them diamond material. But we weren't born yesterday—and why the market continues to expect us to fuel the increasing costs by buying at extortionate prices is beyond me. Yes, we do feel a tad exploited for all the profits you've gained, but we're no suckers. So, no thanks. I'll pass on the avocado toast.[17]

Speaking of consumerism, we've really shaken up the norm here. Our millennial mindset of co-sharing has

---

[17] Note to avocado: I'm sorry. I do love you, but money can only buy so much. And I'm developing a guilt complex, particularly when I eat you sitting on my shitty couch, in my dire inner city flat. You my friend, have unfortunately fallen off the list of consumable priorities. Blame the farmers. Soz.

really influenced these services and demand across the globe. Look at us making the best of a bad economy. We've brought our preference for low cost, ease, sense of community, safety and lifestyle as big factors in shaping this growth. We're bringing a refreshing change to services and influencing consumerism yet again. Credit to us. Boom.

Despite the odd criticism about our 'lack of thoughts regarding retirement' or 'inability to save', inferring that we'll all be living in cardboard boxes on the street—which given the current abodes some of us are living in, isn't going to make that much of a difference—we millennials are not bad with our money or avoid thinking about retirement. The reality is, the financial pressures we face today impact us greatly. I'm not being irresponsible with money or avoiding the inevitable. I do care about how much I can save, but realistic about my plans for retirement. That is, managing my current state of affairs without sacrificing my wants and needs for living in the now. The reward for this? I'll be having long conversations with friends and family when I'm retired, about all the amazing life experiences I've had—and will continue to have.

As for all those other things that continue to get littered across my path that continue to test my patience—well, to that I say, 'bring it'. Not because I like putting up with a constant pain in my arse, but because I realise, at some point, it will be us millennials, having the last laugh— while we're all sitting back drinking fine champagne and eating gluten-free-vegan-fusion hors d'oeuvres. You won't fool or deny this little black duck from getting on and living life.

Millennial darlings. This time is ours. Let's make the most of it. Cheers.

#Shaking up the economy. Boom

CHAPTER 4

Pick Me! Pick Me! Instant Gratification Syndrome Exposed

—————◦—————

But I wasn't sexting. I was simply having a conversation. The fact that it was an exchange of explicit and suggestive messages, mostly about having a threesome with her and another woman and how excited I was by the thought, is irrelevant. Besides, it's not like it's real, or I'm doing anything wrong. It's just texts, and words don't mean anything, right?'

Ok, let's hold up here for a minute. Rewind.

Yes, our world is changing. The advancements of technology over recent decades has revolutionised the speed, access and attainment of information. After the invention of blogging in the 1990s, social media began to explode in popularity. While sites like Myspace and LinkedIn gained prominence in the early 2000s, things ramped up—and quickly. Since Mark Zuckerberg kicked off the Facebook trend (and empire) in 2004, the world has seen the popularity of social media surge. Riding off Zuckerberg's vibe, entrepreneur tech gurus have since followed suit, launching innovative apps such as Youtube (2005), Twitter (2006), Tumblr (2007), WhatsApp (2009), Pinterest (2010), Instagram (2010), the once let's-photograph-and-talk-about-genitalia-and-sex via Snapchat (2011), and Tinder (2012). Today, social media is expanding global connection and cohesion at rapid rates – arguably unprecedented.

On face value, this appears fine. No problem, right? We're just 'movin' with the times'. In fact, we could tip our hat to developers, say, 'Yes, you can thank us millennials for your success' and stick out our hand for a cut of the billions being made. Not least because we've been a successful target market, but now the largest demographic of users.

However, at what point did technology start to change the fundamentals of our relationships? Imposing against our human values and morals; opening and allowing for excuses, for justifications of behaviour, challenging our morals, values and the longevity and substance of our relationships? The world is full of addictions, and technology is now one of them. Although it isn't just about the technology per se, it's about all the add-ons that come with its use. Add-ons that don't come in the form of T&Cs for us to mull over before deciding whether to use a certain technology platform or app. That approach would be considered too backward, too archaic, in fact simply too slow in today's fast paced world that we're all madly trying to catch our breath to keep up with. Besides, with Google and Siri on standby, each of us can spend a few minutes googling the risks and side effects to becoming completely dependent on technology, right? But we don't. So, the technology virus creeps into our minds and bodies, drip feeding us until becoming an unfashionable full flow through our veins. The problem? Millennials are suffering the wrath.

Let's begin . . .

Millennials have grown up in an era teeming with tech. We are the first generation to have been raised with computers and smartphones. We've seen the birth of social media and were the first peeps to accept and nurture this once upon a time infant, into the monopoly it has become. We've seen and experienced media moguls merging and are everyday experts in seeking out the answers to just about every question via the internet.

For us, in today's ever demanding and time-consuming world, the ability to be able to check in, say hello or reach out to anyone in a short, simple and relatively time efficient way via one of many thousand apps is of huge benefit. For most of us, time is of the essence, and technology has provided us with a fantastic way to do more, with less. Less time, less effort, less . . . brain power. We've essentially become multi-tasking gurus, even if at the expense of our thumbs and what others may perceive as laziness. Not laziness to us millennials of course: it's being smart. Who doesn't want to avoid long queues, overcrowded supermarkets, noisy eateries and sardine-can-public transport and sit in the comfort of their own home, avoiding any public interface and the requirements of putting on presentable clothing to accommodate said interface, and instead, with the click of a button—poof! The online genie just fulfilled our online order wishes and all we need to do is wait for the Minions to deliver. If that's not one of the smartest, best time and sanity saving developments, then I don't know what is. Genius, right?

Aside from the convenience factor, and before we get into ripping apart the real impacts of technology, we must give credit where credit is due. And that my friends, is the fact that good old tech has helped mould us into the fabulous human beings we are. How? Technology has put the world into the palm of our hands. And the simple fact is that all the exposure we've had, all that creeping up over time, the not-so-softly-softly approach has given us a fantastic mind and qualities to be proud of. Qualities that appear au naturel, however, have been helped by tech.

#Open minded and informed

Technology has made us open minded and informed, not to mention savvy, critical thinkers. The information age has exposed us to many sides of the world: from politics, to economics, to business, you name it. And every happening and development we have witnessed in our life has given us the skill of being able to stand and think on our own two feet, and where needed, bring new perspective to the table of any situation. Being connected with the world has also given us the belief that we can do anything we set our mind too: we can be, do or have anything we want, and that technology will not just make it possible, but a lot easier to achieve.

#Adaptability

Technology is constantly evolving. We only need to reflect on the past year to see how it adapts and alters at an incredible rate. By default, we millennials have learnt how to adapt to technology changes easily and in most cases, readily. What this has created is a generation that is incredibly adaptable and flexible; a generation who knows how to roll with the punches so to speak. Ready to call 'Next!' This is arguably one of the qualities we tend to forget about. So, when we are hit with those pain in the arse moments or challenging periods, rather than reflecting and drawing down on this strength, we instead put on our victim hat (yes, you know who you are).

#Driving evolution

Further to the obvious benefit of growing up with ever-changing technology is that we not only expect change, and can move with change, but we make change happen. We are a driving force behind the advances in technology, not just because we're the biggest consumers of technology (alongside Gen Z), but because we're demanding advances. Think same day services, like Amazon Prime, or Click-and-Collect. These advances have resulted in devices, apps and technology that offer us more flexibility. Our phone is a prime example. Once upon a time we were happy with a smartphone as it was; but why settle for just a device that sends texts, emails and calls when we can buy, sell, invest, plan, search and do most of our daily tasks with the same thing? Think about it. We only need look at the development of smartphones to see how they have dramatically shaped the way we view technology. Computers, telephones, calculators, MP3 players, maps, cameras, video recorders, clocks and notepads are now contained in one handheld device. Brilliant.

#Efficient

Despite the odd slander we get every now and then, millennials aren't stupid. Especially when it comes to tech. We know how to play the game and to make technology work for us in just about all areas of our life. When was the last time you *didn't* consult your phone for something you needed, knowing that it would solve whatever it was in the half the time and effort it would take *without* it? Having said that, we do recognise that technology can't solve all our problems—yet, that is (bring on the 'robot revolution' and we'll be investing in personal robots, pronto).

Growing up in the digital age has introduced a drastic difference in the ways in which common things are done. The internet has created faster, more efficient ways in doing nearly everything. As a result, we've become incredibly efficient—super-efficient in some cases—and we translate that into all parts of our life.

#Distance has been redefined

Nothing is too far away. Well, we don't see distance as 'distance' per se. Because we're always connected and have the world at our fingertips, whoever or whatever we want is just a stone's throw away.

#One step forward, two steps back

The downside to all this pizzazz technology is the bind that it places us in—and not the Fifty Shades of Grey type. It's the balancing act that most of us millennials are unfortunately failing at: balancing our use of technology.

One of the biggest problems that underpins this, is that technology has been a given in our lives from birth. Not to today's standard of course, where Gen Z babies are practically born holding an iPhone, but the use of technology in some way has always been there. Computers started to find their way into the home in 1975: admittedly a massive box that took up half the size of a room or became the centre piece of the house. Those 'brick' mobile phones that existed once upon a time, were only in 1983—meaning that the youngest of us at that time were three years old (give or take). Over time, we were exposed to a brand-new world of technology, that fast became our norm.

The bittersweet taste that we're currently experiencing is manyfold. Which means it's not simple; in fact, the layers of complexity tend to run a little deeper than we care to acknowledge. Technology has always been intended to make the world a better place, and in some parts has. The downside is, it's developing and evolving at such rapid paces that it's outgrowing human evolution. Yes. I'm not just referring here to robots and artificial intelligence advancements that have redefined the human position in the world. But the fact that technology in all its glory, is surpassing our mental capacities to keep up. We're being teaching to sprint, before we can even pick up a light jog. As a result, it's our brains that are suffering. Quite literally.

But before we get in to exploring the brain drain, let's start by looking at the vehicle that's become the catalyst to technology addictions for us. The smartphone. Millennials are the largest adopters of this form of technology; in fact, in 2015, 86 percent of 18 to 29-year-olds owned a smartphone.[18]

The growing problem we all have of this reliance on our smartphones, is becoming quite possibly the world's next crisis: smartphone dystopia. You only need to lift your head and look around to see the effect. For most of us, our phones have become an extension of our bodies; if not a body part itself. We love our phones for good reason – but the qualities we find most appealing and useful are the ones that adversely impact us - and our minds. Think about it. We love the constant connectivity we have with the world: but have lost the ability to sit comfortably with our own company, with ourselves. In fact, the mere

---

[18] Anderson, M. 2015. *Technology Device Ownership: 2015*. Pew Research Center, U.S.

thought alone is enough to frighten us. 'But what will I do?', 'Who will I talk to?', 'What if I don't like myself?', 'What if I lose my mind?'. All valid questions of course – for someone suffering from a first-degree addiction (note to self). The multitude of apps that exist – which collectively could solve just about every 'first world' problem we have – make us revert back to childhood glee, however our dependency has clouded our memory of the times when we had to plan, prioritise and god forbid, make a concerted effort to get shit done. The responsiveness, the fact that we can have every question answered in a second, is magic—but as a result, we've all become annoying Veruca Salt's (I. WANT. IT. NOW.) with Google and Siri our BFF's.

Body parts aside, our phone has practically become a source of our self. Through the constant use and multitude of apps we're constantly engaging and interacting with, our phones have become the link to the wider world. We communicate, translate and record things that define what we think, what we experience in life and who we are. It's a little alarmingly when you think about. This small device, this phone of ours, that has become so utterly powerful in not just influencing, shaping and defining who we are—but *becoming* who we are.

Now, it doesn't take a genius to work out that there are going to be obvious problems with this. Not just from a dependency factor, but from a replacement factor. If the phone has become an extension of the body and the self, then what's happening to the *actual* body and the *actual* self? Let's turn our heads to researchers,[19] who are already one step ahead.

Issue 1: Reduction in brain cells and mental skills

Research has identified significant psychological effects from our dependence on our phones and tech. First, we have the brain drain issue. Literally. What studies are showing, is that the more we've integrated smartphones into our lives, the more our brains have suffered. Think vital mental skills like learning, logical reasoning, problem solving, abstract thought and creativity.

---

[19] Stothart, C., Mitchum, A., and Yehnert, C. (2015). The attentional cost of receiving a cell phone notification. *Journal of Experimental Psychology: Human Perception and Performance* 41(4), 893-897; Ward, A.F., Duke, K., Gneezy, A., and Bos., M.W. (2017). Brain Drain: The Mere Presence of One's Own Smartphone Reduces Available Cognitive Capacity. *Journal of Association for Consumer Research* 4(2), 140-154. The University of Chicago Press.

Essential skills that are being put on the back burner, causing brain cells to literally fall of the perch and die.

Issue 2: Forgetting what's real

With this, is also the distorted reality syndrome. Ok, so maybe not quite distorted, but our inability to distinguish knowledge we keep in our head from the information that we find on our phones. What this means is that we're essentially not learning anything at all. Our constant Googling is showing us information quick smart – and we don't have to do anything to retain it, because if we forget, we ask Google again. Check your search history. How many times have you asked the same question, or looked up the same thing more than once? What this means is that we're sacrificing our ability to turn information into knowledge. We're great at getting the data but lose the meaning because of our inability to learn. We could beg the question as to whether this is creating more storage in our brains because of the in-and-out data that's syphoning through at rapid paces. Sadly, it's unlikely. With the demise of brain cells, reduction in mental skills and absence of learning, our brains are more likely going to end up resembling Jell-O than a well-rounded functioning organ.

Issue 3: Anxiety complexes

The psychological element to all of this, is the fact we've developed anxiety complexes and attachments that far override all health boundaries. Research has shown that a simple inability to answer the phone causes spikes in blood pressure, pulse rates and a decline in problem-solving skills. [20] Now, you and I both know you're guilty of this. Think about the last time you heard your phone ring, or received a text or email, hearing the 'bing', and couldn't get to your phone in time. Did it make your heart rate increase? Just a little? Not to mention that you, and the other 90 percent of us, have likely experienced the phantom vibration syndrome or phantom ringing syndrome (aka 'ringxiety'), where we've thought or 'felt' our phone vibrating or ringing when it wasn't. Indicating that we've become individuals who are living in a state of heightened awareness and sensitivity: triggered very easily.

---

[20] Ibid, 140-154.

Issue 4: Vacant and distracted

Coupled with the anxiety factor, is the fact that being on high alert means we are also living in a state where we aren't fully present when we are with someone—especially when having a conversation. It's like we're there, but not *quite* there, as our phones are reminding us of all the people we could (and are currently) chatting with electronically. Think about the last in-person conversation you had with someone where your mind didn't drift to think about your phone, or you checked your phone while being with that person. Even right now, as you're reading this chapter, I can guarantee that you haven't once not been distracted. Think about the couples you see at restaurants, or families in fast food outlets, all distracted by their phones and paying no real attention to their company. The result? Conversations and interactions are much shallower and less satisfying than they could be because we just aren't 'there'.

The simple solution would be to remove all phones from us, like naughty children being reprimanded; but the reality is, it's not just our phones that are having an impact. Without the functions they have—i.e. connecting us to the world through the web and apps—then they'd be relatively useless devices. More broadly, technology has introduced bigger fish to fry.

#Need-it-now mentality

As humans, we're hardwired to want things. It's not uncommon, or unusual. In fact, if we didn't want things in life, then we'd be living a rather boring-as-bat-shit existence. Nothing to look forward to, nothing to trigger excitement, nothing to work towards, no goals, no plans . . . you get the picture. But it's not just things we want, it's all the good things, nice things, things that make us feel *good*. This want to feel pleasure (aka the 'pleasure principle') is what typically drives our behaviour in seeking to gratify our needs, wants and urges. These wants, needs and urges can be as simple or complex as we like, but the one thing we all have in common, is we want, whatever it is, *pronto*. And when we don't get what we want, or are able to find fulfilment, we turn into anxious, tense and irritable people. Yes, you know it.

Now, growing up as kids, we were all subjected to the principle of patience and having to wait. Think about the supermarket temper tantrum after being denied sweets. Parents yanking us by the wrist, dragging us along the floor, us, red faced and screaming, covered in snot and tears—all because we wanted something and were told either 'No', or 'Wait'. A classic child and parent milestone of devastation and humiliation. Yes, we were being taught invaluable life skills at the time—but the fact that everything seemed to take forever to get, gave us spilt milk complexes. Regardless of being put through the motions of impulse control, restraint and emotional resilience testing, underneath it all, it didn't change the fact that we wanted it now. All we did was wrap those babes in cotton wool and nurse them with TLC until the arrival of technology: which ripped off the cover with force and pillaged our self-restraint.

Introducing Instant Gratification Syndrome (IGS): the not-so-new accessory for millennials. IGS is as it sounds: a syndrome, a condition, an illness and even an addiction. The instant gratification aspect isn't the issue, it's when it becomes out of control and you end up in a world of hurt that you didn't know existed, until after the fact. IGS isn't something we get stung with either; it tends to seep into our skin, into our blood, becoming a part of us before we start to show symptoms. Think of it like any addiction. It always starts somewhere. Softy, softy until . . . bang!

There are those of us millennials who might be more conscious of the fact that there is a before and after technology effect especially with IGS. All we need to do is look back at our childhood, or teens, to see how technology has influenced our reactions and emotions to just about everything in life. In fact, alarmingly so in some cases.

Let me share with you a story: 1999 was the year when the now well-loved PC was introduced to my family home. Ironic, given the fact this was also the year which spawned the Millennium Bug fever (in hindsight a huge overreaction). The novelty of having a computer was huge. Computers were a privileged item back then and only reserved for schools, or workplaces. Of course, you'd hear the odd rumour every now and then that some classmate or kid in school had just got their hands on one—which would spark a tad of jealously. I mean at that age, thinking about having Pac-Man in the family home was incredibly appealing. This wasn't of course, to take the glee from the fact that gaming had already occurred. In fact, many a weekend had already been spent in sheer frustration with the ongoing connectivity issues with the Atari (with the rest of the world seemingly also annoyed as discontinuation occurred in 1992), followed by upgrades to the Nintendo 64, and only due to persistent begging, the Sony PlayStation. And while there was nothing wrong at the time with growing up with Donkey Kong, Mario Brothers and Sonic the Hedgehog, there was something about the computer that opened a new possibility: connection with the world. Hello, World Wide Web.

It was like a million Christmases at once, with a shiny new toy to play with—albeit taking up some serious space in the house. Now, at the tender age of 14, one could rightly assume that there's a level of innocence, an absence of maturity on how to safely navigate what was essentially, the keys to the world. No real knowledge of what would happen when online and suddenly 'out there'. Or, what would be found. Internet security and parenting controls weren't something that was talked about and only really become an issue after the fact of some drastic event (i.e. R-rated movies being freely accessible, and children being exposed to porn). The glow of having a computer tended to override the other issues that the future world in hindsight, could have better mitigated. The world was a different place back then.

Somewhat more sheltered, somewhat more protected because the internet hadn't unleashed its wrath of exposing every nook and cranny and every dirty secret hiding in the dark.

To enhance our connectivity with others, we were introduced to instant messaging platforms; a service which has flooded the world and, in some parts, become the critical linking factor in our relationships. Think back to MSN Messenger. The platform that introduced us to the start of instant gratification and commenced our dependency on tech. Call it what you will, but there was an element of 'Dating in the Dark' back then—no matter what age. Chat rooms had become the norm—a virtual place for people anywhere in the world to hang out. All you needed to do to gain permission was create a username and password. No need to set up a profile, no need to be verified, no need to display a photo: a blind talking with the blind approach to conversation and friendships. Seemingly innocent, until we realised it created a potential feeding ground for child sex fetishes and offenders.

His name was Rob: A 25-year-old male teacher, working with special needs kids. He said he liked to run marathons and raise money for 'those in need'. He lived with his mother, who was dependent on his care as she had a disability, but he was determined to move out one day when he could afford to put her in care. He confessed to not have many friends, as his commitments prevented him from meeting people. Nice enough guy.

Me: A 14-year-old, grade 9 primary school student who had recently hit puberty. No experience with boys, other than pop star poster crushes and lacked friendships because of shyness. Lacking significant attention in the family home and struggling to even remotely like herself, but overall trusting the good will of others. Rob became my first virtual friend, and coupled with MSN messenger, the instant gratification seed planter.

Nightly MSN chat room appearances became the norm: 7 pm for 30 minutes, except for weekends. Then over a series of weeks, it became twice a day, morning and night, before moving into weekends. I felt attached: not to him, but to the pleasure and delight I was getting out of this brand-new world. The sound of the 'dings', the flash on the screen, the texts to read. The novelty was, by all accounts, continuing to grow. I'd made a few other brief virtual friends, exchanged the odd 'Hi, how R U?' texts which was nice, but not as much as I liked the exchanges I had with my friend Rob. However, the reality was, shit was brewing underneath: new tech + excitement + attention that at the time I was lacking, opened the pathway to fulfilment and feelings of pleasure, and an unhealthy dependency. I would check the clock each night, check how many texts he sent me, measure the time in between, sit with bated breath after his 'BRB' replies. Anxious and often irritable.

It wasn't until a few months had passed that I realised something was off with Rob. Call it a puberty epiphany, but I'd suddenly realised that my virtual friendship with Rob was a sham. Not only did Rob send me lacy underwear for my 15th birthday, ask me to wear it and send him a photo, but he invited me to stay with him at a 'surprise location'. Now, I might have been an innocent 14-year-old teenage being fuelled by the need of instant gratification, but I wasn't a fool. Rob was a potential paedophile and I dodged bullet.

Now, child grooming stories aside, there's a point. Two in fact. First, is to demonstrate how vulnerable children are. But not just children in general; millennial children (i.e. us) who were introduced to a whole new world without having got a handle on the existing. Thrust into a new mode of operation, a new way of communication before we'd ever fully grasped the soft skills needed for in-person interaction and more importantly, being able to set boundaries. Second, how the impacts of technology start planting their seeds much, much earlier than we'd ever imagined. Setting up a new foundation, a new way of becoming, being led like a donkey following a carrot on a stick, into the depths of something unknown and unexpected: affecting our state of being, our wellbeing, our mental health—our whole operation as a human being.

What started as harmless, became harmful—for some of us more than others. And like moths drawn to a flame, we couldn't deter from the shiny new objects in front of us. The glee and excitement no different from anything else that felt rewarding to us or built up our anticipation. The only exception has been the subsequent programming that we've all undergone to expect immediate feedback. Thank you, technology.

#Influenced by society

While to some degree we can choose what we see, read and hear online, the choice tends to come about after we've been bombarded with information – and sometimes too late. We find ourselves sifting through the ego, opinions and attitudes of others. The latest trends are forced upon us. The general consensus of what's normal and what's not, who's liked and who's not, what's right and what's wrong . . . it's an epidemic. Waiting for us to comment or make judgment, to agree with the rest of society as it collectively creates division and boundaries; once upon a time nonexistent until each of us decided to agree and provide validation along with the rest of society. Consumerism is heightened. As are societal expectations. Advertisement after advertisement presented about the latest must have gadget or breakthrough diet.

What comes with this—and what is one crippling issue for us millennials—is that society starts portraying all these fabulous things, all this amazing potential, and like excited children we are drawn to everything because we are creatures of optimism and see opportunity in everything. The result is, we end up at a crossroad of endless choices and possibilities that we find so bewildering that we freeze up.

It's like going into a restaurant and being offered a long menu. It's painstaking for some of us who mull over the potential in every dish: if it's healthy, if it's full of carbs, if it's gluten free, vegan free, taste free, if it's in our price range, if it'll stretch the budget, if we've been to the gym and deserve it, if we're having said item in the next week, if we've had it this week, if we're having other dinners out, if that dinner will be somewhere pricey or cheap, if it'll have the same food type because we don't want to spend money on the same thing, if we even feel like eating out . . . you get the picture.

What do we do? We either freeze to a holt and do nothing, essentially becoming stuck, or we have someone make the decision for us. Whether it be our dinner date or society, the vulnerable state of being we millennials find ourselves in, becomes incredibly perplexing. In fact, so much so, that we start to fear making the wrong decision, so end up in state of despair, crying 'Help me!'

#Forgetting who we are

Sometimes, despite how tough we are and how much resilience we have, social media can become all too overwhelming. So overwhelming that we can feel lost. Our energy and our uniqueness saturated with what is essentially, the BS of the world. We find ourselves feeling a touch vague or lost, as the ongoing exposure starts to remove us from who we are. Creating a sense of disconnection to ourselves because we have been lured into the fray of what can feel like a rabid society: attached to everything else but the people that we are. To add fuel to the fire, is of course that while this is happening—a part of why this is happening—is that our self-confidence, self-esteem and self-worth suffer. Each time we check our social media accounts, view the posts, photos and opinions of others, we start the comparison game. Not deliberately in most cases, but when the glitz and glamour of everyone's 'perfect side' is being spewed across social media, how do we not?

#External validation becomes the norm

While the odd thought about how our life shapes up compared to our friends or family every now and then could probably be considered normal, the slope starts to become slippery when we start secretly assessing the number of likes, re-tweets or comments. Let's be honest, you'd be lying if you said you hadn't checked those figures—both on your own posts and that of others. Again, perfectly reasonable once or twice, but the risk for us—one which is incredibly high—is that we start to become dependent on the attention and validation we get from others. Going back to IGS, it's a momentary high that is short-lived, and if we're too attached to this state of being, we find that the come down is quick to appear—leaving us feeling worse off than we were before. Especially, god forbid, if we don't reach that imaginary number we have in our heads about what constitutes acceptance, or dare I say 'success'. Often completely skewed because we spend too much time following people like the Kardashians who have billions of followers, and for some ludicrous reason, attach this to the notion of being successful. Come on peeps, wake up now.

#Dating becomes a game

He's just not that into you . . . or is he? She's replied 'LMAO' to a text you sent her, which means you're in . . . or are you? Technology has changed the dating game, hands down. Literally. It's become a task that is largely being navigated by our hands, finger swipes and check ins. It's made dating appear simple, yet incredibly complicated at the same time. Technology today presents us with more options than we ever thought possible. For those in the market, we are offered a smorgasbord of potential candidates that we can sift through like dirty laundry. While it might seem like a cracking good deal to come across, the downside is it's made our relationships superficial and incredibly disposable. On the superficial level, with so much choice out there, we've become a generation of honing in on the nth detail of another: 'He doesn't have a nice enough smile', 'Her skin looks a little yellow in that light', 'I can't see his full body, but his face doesn't make him look overweight', 'Those lips are gorgeous on her, but her eyes are a centimetre too far apart. Pity'.

We start analysing and judging people based on their looks, before we've even had a chance to say hello. And for those that may not quite fit the bill of what we want on a physical level, any interactions we have with them are already biased. Our first conversations don't happen over coffee; they happen over text, or an app, in a setting that removes all ability to read a person's body language or emotion. Those of us who may be little shy end up building a relationship based purely on text—because who doesn't feel more comfortable and more at ease saying things by text than face to face? We can put on a mask behind a screen and pretend to be anyone we want. The problem is that things often turn pear shaped when you do have the in-person meet and realise you can't maintain a conversation because you've either forgotten how to converse, or you've shared every detail already by text, leaving nothing to talk about. So, we leave our date with our tail between our legs and go back to the drawing board. Ten minutes later, we're back online, doing it all over again. The same process, the same cycle.

Yes, in a world where we're all suffering from an absence of time, dating apps have admittedly added to the convenience factor of our lives—at least helping with the initial meet and greet. But at the end of the day, we are still human and the meaning that we get out of our relationships stems beyond technology. Which means that if we're wanting something a little more substantial with our potential partnerships or dating affairs, we're going to have to brush up on our people skills and make time for authentic conversation. If not, we run the risk of contributing to fuelling a data and tech world full of meaningless superficial pursuits and in turn, causing us more sleepless nights than not. Sex not included.

So how do we fix us?

Millennial Survival Techniques

Millennials, if we're wanting to be the bigger person in our technology and smartphone relationships, then we've a heck of a ladder to climb—at least for most of us.

There is no blame game in this; it is simply the way we've been raised—in a world of tech that has influenced us to great degrees. The positive is that we've become quite a storm to be reckoned with. We will continue to keep marketing gurus and tech developers on their toes, and in the game, because it's us that's running the show, right? We have an insatiable appetite for knowing, learning, growing and are by far the most open-minded folk you'll come across. No topic is off limit, there is nothing taboo and we have technology to thank for that — for opening our eyes, our minds and our hearts to more: to possibility, to potential, to having, being and doing whatever it is we set out minds to. A world of connection and unlimited information. We keep people on their toes, because we've been kept on our toes — moving with the times of tech, we've become smarter, more empowered and more educated along the way. And what we have to offer people in our lives, and the world, is of huge value. Check the earlier list again and tell me you don't think we have something of great substance to add to this planet? Yes, we are fabulous.

But the downside is, too many of us millennials out there are suffering with issues surrounding technology that could have been avoided, should we have been given a guidebook on the release of every new tech development or invention. We've not been sheltered from the storm, we've had to weather it and for some of us, we've been hit hard. But it doesn't mean we need to resort to living on a desert island with Tom Hanks, washed up on shore with our own personal Wilson, seething with anxiety, uncertainty and fear. No, no, no. All it means is rather than wait for the ship to come in, we make our own life raft and set back to the sea. Yes, it might be difficult given there'll be no internet to Google 'how to build a life raft', but we're adventurers at heart and will use the journey as another achievement to add to that backpack of trophies and ribbons that we have—and then contact Bear Grylls to reiterate our survival.

The reality is, we are going to continue to suck up, like a dry sponge, the daily bombardment and saturation of other peoples' lives, if we don't take off our blindfolds. We will continue to compare our lives with others, placing judgment, feeling like failures, succumbing to pressure and expectation, losing our sense of confidence, self-worth and validation if we don't put on our big person boots and step up to the plate of batting for our own team. Batting for ourselves. Our ego is going to come a crop if we continue to swim in the shallow waters of society and get caught up in the tides of societal BS and the expectations of the rest of the world. It's a fact. It will be move over Alice, while we take her place and fall headfirst down the rabbit hole.

We need to take the time to stop for a moment; take an un-technological breath and just simply be with ourselves. Sit in the content of our company, without anything else. For those of you gems who can't even fathom the thought of what that might look like, let alone feel like, because tech is so much a part of your blood that without it, you might as well keel over . . . then all I say is challenge yourself—because what you're currently doing is handing over all power to a device. Your phone and tech are driving you: controlling your thoughts, actions and emotions and making all sorts of turns in your life that you don't need, or in fact want.

While we like to credit ourselves for innovation and being the leaders of change, there's a whole new industry out there that's been created thanks to the tech fuelled world and our inability to sort this shit out: the digital detox industry. The birth of this industry is a catch 22. A service much needed in today's society of social media and technology obsessions, but appalling given the hefty profit these places are making off those of us in our generation who are, or are on the verge of addiction et al. We're living in an era where we're already strapped for cash and missing out on investments let alone having to consider throwing money into retreats that switch our 'on' button 'off' for a few days. Something that if we take the time to reflect on, and make a concerted effort, can do ourselves.

The world isn't going to get any better if we keep plugging away with our obsessions with tech. Millennials, it's time to start looking at life through your own eyes, rather than the lens of an iPhone.

#Do your brain a favour

CHAPTER 5

Hi, I'm a Millennial and I'm a Stressaholic

———————○———————

Newsflash: Millennials are less keen to get 'hammered, high, or horizontal' compared to previous generations,[21] but their mental health is falling apart—Humpty Dumpty style.

Now, any savvy business entrepreneur would be quick to link the dots and take out shares in the pharmaceutical industry or start monopolising in private practice clinics. Let's face it, based on that startling fact, there are some mega bucks to be made from the current state of being of our mental health. Not by us of course. Heck, our purse strings are pulled tighter each day by the pitiful state of affairs, and we're not living in the same world as Charlie Brown, lucky enough to be consulting Lucy for five cents

---

[21] Millennials are less keen than previous generations on illicit drugs. *The Economist*. 2017.

a pop. We're living in cash strapped times with no guaranteed ROI on anything, let alone our mental health—unless we can get our shit together in the meantime.

The days when talking about mental health was a taboo topic, hidden in the closet alongside sexuality, are behind us. Today, it's a hard to avoid the topic, especially if you're part of our generation. It's not from a favouritism point of view either. While mental health challenges have become more publicised and topical, making it easy to have 'those conversations', for some of us, these issues per se, have become our bread and butter. Taking a comfortable position in our back pockets and driving us into states of despair.

Studies are repeatably showing that millennials are at a higher risk of mental health issues, than any other generation. We're experiencing unprecedented levels of anxiety and depression, making us quite literally a 'generation on edge'. Our sense of wellbeing across areas of health, relationships, and finances is low. We are becoming more and more socially isolated, suffering significant drops in personal wellbeing. Even our sense of belonging has plummeted by over 30 percent in the last decade,[22] enough to offend our red-glitter suited Sister Sledge[23] fans as we aren't feeling part of a family.

You don't need to be Einstein to work out the reasons why. Not when we look at the reality of the world through the millennial lens. We are the first generation in the modern era to have higher levels of student loan debt, poverty, unemployment and lower levels of wealth and personal income, than any other generation at the same stage of life. Housing unaffordability slaps us in the face every day, as does the rising cost of living. The chains of societal pressures, ideals and expectations loom over our heads, with just enough force to make us feel stuck—and in some cases, with chains around our ankles. Social media does no favours in encouraging us to compare ourselves to others; self-esteem and self-worth walking the plank, ready to jump at any moment, increasing body image crisis and feelings of inadequacy. All these challenges and issues leading to rising levels of anxiety, stress, depression, eating disorders and addictions:

---

[22] Kingman. D. 2018. New IF research shows that young adults' wellbeing has fallen by 10% since mid-1990s. Intergenerational Foundation, U.K.
[23] *We are Family* was the 1978 hit released by American band Sister Sledge.

berating our mental health. It's no wonder there are plenty of us out there in the world hitting the unfashionable quarter-life crises 'milestone' at the speed of light. Desperately trying to find any means possible to bring some form of sanity back and provide a sense of self.

But I'm jumping ahead with the summary version—the obvious version. To understand the *actual* situation, we need to get under the covers of the not-so-warm duvet and explore the nitty gritty elements of the 'why', the 'how' and the 'how the hell do we fix this?' issues.

#A growing crisis? The stats

Anxiety: a crafty old chestnut. Defined as *'a feeling of worry, nervousness, or unease about something with an uncertain outcome'* [24] it has become, for some of us millennials, a state of being. And while enough of a drama queen to handle on its own, it likes to give extra

---

[24] Oxford English Dictionary, 'Anxiety'. Oxford University Press, 2019. https://en.oxforddictionaries.com/
On a side note, the following exert appeared under the definition of 'Anxiety': *anxieties about the moral decline of today's youth*. Moral decline? Did we miss the memo? Obviously, this definition wasn't written by a millennial.

bang for buck by partnering itself with the blues: depression.

The stats speak volumes. At least one in five, or 20 percent of us, will report depression in the workplace.[25] Studies show that we are the most anxious generation, especially women,[26] with up to three-quarters of us feeling somewhat or extremely anxious about paying our bills.[27] And if you're living in the U.S. and are either in college, or have graduated in the last few years, you're more than likely to have been, or are, one of the five million students who are suffering from mental health concerns.[28] In fact in 2014, 61 percent of you may have reported feeling overwhelming anxiety within the last year and 35.5 percent reported feeling so depressed that it was difficult to function.[29] In 2015, 25 percent of you would have been treated for a diagnosable mental illness.[30] Professionals have even declared that 'the

[25] McCreary, M. 2015. Anxiety and work: The impact of anxiety on different generations of employees. Morneau Shepell, U.S.
[26] APA Public Opinion Poll – Annual Meeting 2018. American Psychiatric Association. 2018. https://www.psychiatry.org
[27] Ibid.
[28] Gruttadaro, D., and Crudo, D. 2012. *College Students Speak: A Survey Report on Mental Health*. The National Alliance on Mental Illness, U.S.
[29] Ibid.
[30] Ibid.

average high school kid today has the same level of anxiety as the average psychiatric patient in the early 1950s.'[31] Which might explain why the suicide rate among young adults has tripled since the 1950s, with it being the second most common cause of death among college students.[32]

Then we have the lifestyle factors: eating patterns, sexual activity, sleeping and drinking. While we've taken things down a notch from the days of hippies, psychedelics and punk raving, we can't escape the evidence showing increasing maladaptive patterns of behaviour. While sleep deprivation may have sounded cool once upon a time, it's not anymore. It brings with it a bucket load of associated problems, including the brinks of insanity (just ask Randy Gardner[33]). Disordered eating has also been documented to be on the rise. While studies in the 1980s

---

[31] Leahy, R.L. 2008. How Big a Problem Is Anxiety? *Psychology Today*. https://www.psychologytoday.com
[32] Henriques, G. 2014. The College Student Mental Health Crisis Today's college students are suffering from an epidemic of mental illnesses. *Psychology Today*. https://www.psychologytoday.com
[33] Randy Gardner is the record holder for the longest time a human has gone without sleep: 11 days and 25 minutes. Cognitive and behavioural changes were observed, including moodiness, problems with short term memory and concentration, paranoia, and hallucinations.

suggested a 4 to 5 percent prevalence of eating disorders in college students, it quadrupled to 20 per cent by 2006.[34] A phenomenal finding that suggests we're using means of starving, purging, binging or excessive dieting or exercise to deal with life stress. While patterns of sexual behaviours across the world vary, the emergence of our seemingly 'hook up' culture—one largely supported by social media—has had the finger pointed at it for being linked to psychological problems, such as drinking, anxiety and depression. The prevalence of sexually transmitted diseases increasing anxiety and depression and drinking contributing to what has become a rise in alcohol abuse, dependence, binge drinking and driving while intoxicated,[35] not to mention sexual assaults and violence.

What the?!

---

[34] Statistics and Research on Eating Disorders. The National Eating Disorders Association, U.S. 2018.
https://www.nationaleatingdisorders.org.
[35] Studies in the U.S. report up to 30 percent of college students meet the criteria for a diagnosis of abuse and 6 percent for alcohol dependence. Knight, J.R., Weschler, H., Kuo, M., Seibring, M., Weitzman, E.R., and Schuckit, M.A. (2015). Alcohol abuse and dependence among U.S. college students. *Journal of Studies on Alcohol* 63(3), 263–270.

Ok, so on face value it reads as if we're living in a dog-eat-dog world, or some weird Simon Pegg movie that involves a looming zombie attack or the world combusting because of the combined stress exerted from millennial brains around the world. However, while it may feel like a doom and gloom story, it's not. In fact, once you've become aware of the 'why' and the 'how', you'll likely be donning a superman cape and taking the world on—Kenny Powers style.

#But darling, what do you mean be natural? I *am* natural

If we received a dollar for every time, we answered the question 'How are you?' with 'Great' or 'I'm fine', we'd be rich. But fake rich: money earnt through lies and dishonesty that would weigh down on our virtuous hearts like a ton of bricks, to the point we'd probably give it back. However, what we have developed—virtues or not—is a surprising ability to look like we've got our shit together. It's called 'duck syndrome': a state where we're all struggling yet trying to appear like we're not struggling. Think about it from a visual: Picture a duck swimming across a lake. On the surface, the duck seems to be gliding along effortlessly. However, beneath the surface, the duck's webbed feet are busy paddling to keep itself afloat—frantic, fraught and desperate. But no one second guesses the duck or what's going on under the surface. Just as no one second guesses the façade we've come to put up—fooling just about everyone, including ourselves. The problem with this state of being, is that other than being incredibly exhausting, it reflects a perception that being honest in our feelings of anxiety or overwhelm aren't acceptable. Which also includes being honest when we're struggling, admitting 'failures' or asking for help. Now, while most of you would probably respond with, 'What utter bollocks,' or 'Come on now, we're living it the 21st century where everyone is like, honest, and shit', the truth is, as much as that ideal sounds fabulous, we've not quite living in an Utopian society.

This fake-it-until-you-make-it persona is important to raise because it sets the scene for many of the reasons as to why we might not know (deliberately, or not) the stark reality of our mental health. So now having got out the fact that we are masters of faking it, we don't have to continue with the façade. And certainly not while reading this book. It's time to get real with ourselves for a moment. All we need to do is open our minds and look at some of the factors at play as to why we are suffering and then, what we can do about it.

#Go you good thing, go! Like being ridden by a jockey . . .

Pressure. That thing that we millennials are good at. Like, *really*, good at. To the point of taking the concept of pressure cooker to the next level (well, almost). And it all goes back to childhood (yes, again). We are the generation that were told by our parents that we could be anything we wanted, so long as we tried hard enough. Add on to the equation our Pavlov-conditioned need for rewards, ultimately becoming a measure of our success—and voila—we're left with some pretty ugly conditions that are responsible for setting the backdrop of our pressure fueled lives.

The university (or college) scene is probably the easiest case in point to illustrate. If you're not there now, go back and think about those good old days of 'repressed freedom'. Studies have found commonalities across students when it comes to reporting levels of anxiety and depression, which are often coming a crop because of pressure. We've had—or have—a hard time balancing responsibility. Turning up to college, completing study hours, working part-time jobs, undertaking internships, participating in clubs, student leadership obligations, maintaining relationships, balancing a social life and dealing with family obligations—the latter, largely being pressure from parents. Which, not surprisingly, has been one of the factors contributing most to the growing levels of anxiety and depression amongst students (and us). Now, I'm not saying this is a blanket rule. Some parents were quite ok with a hands-off approach—although it didn't change the fact that despite this, we still felt a need to measure up. Leading to a 'damned if we do, damned if we don't' situation. Overwhelming, at all?

However post-graduation, it doesn't get any easier. In fact, part of the problem is that the message we get in addition to 'you can be anything you want' is the 'if you work hard enough in life, you're going to be ok'. A statement of false security—offering the guise of a safety blanket that we find out all too quickly, is invisible. In addition to the fact that there are no assurances or guarantees, and quite frankly, working hard in life does not translate into being ok. Far, far from it.

The workplace is a perfect example for this. While the old 'lazy millennial' stereotype still gets thrown at us, studies are now disproving this myth. In fact, across the world, millennials are putting in the hours—even to the detriment of our wellbeing.[36] Culprits, yet again tend to be the same: the obvious reflection of social and economic factors at play. Some of us feel the need to work all hours to have any sort of job security or potentially move up the career ladder—presenting a good argument for whether we've become a generation of hostages. Social media has killed off any downtime, or 'unavailability' to work. Yes, we value work-life balance and we don't want to be working all the time, but let's face it, it's hard to put off replying to a work email until the next day, or after the weekend, unless you uninstall the app. Social media has created a culture where there now exists a pressure to work, or respond, even when we're not at work. Knowingly or not, we tend to fuel the expectation because of the ridiculous bind we find ourselves in with our initiative vs fear personal standoff.

---

[36] Millennial Careers: 2020 Vision. Facts, Figures and Practical Advice from Workforce Experts. Manpower Group. 2016. https;//www.manpowergroup.com.

#What do you mean, failure? There's no such thing, right?

Let's be honest. On reflection, our childhoods never really afforded us the chance to learn what failure was. It wasn't something we considered at the time, because we'd always been under the impression that there really was no such thing. It certainly wasn't a dinner table conversation with our parents. The reality is, we've grown up in a competitive, bell-curve, wait-list society— which by default has placed us in a position where we've had to glove up and fight. From a spot on the sport team, to a place at university or college, to securing a job; leaving us in a constant state of being on edge, feeling defensive and feeling the need to secure a place, a position, or make a stand. We've had to fight, and we continue to fight—which does nothing but add to the undercurrent of anxiety and stress that we're already feeling. Our perception and lack of experiences with failure also opens a can of worms when it comes to the concept of 'struggling'. More specifically, our ability to acknowledge when we are struggling. Why? Because we've not had to struggle, or in some cases, allowed to. Often as kids, our parents stepped in and made things right. But while saving us from having to endure feelings of discomfort and stress, has equally ripped us of the opportunity to understand and experience this state of being.

#No longer feelin' it: Reward depletion

It's no surprise that over-parenting has psychologically affected us, which has manifested in our inability to work out a balance between independent decision making and asking for help. Let's be honest. There have all been times where all we've wanted to do is rock in a corner, suck our thumb and cry—rather than raise our hand and ask for help. Alarmingly, this has—for some of us—affected our sense of reward. Which includes what we feel is rewarding and how we go about achieving it. Studies have shown that for some of us, we've shifted our focus from intrinsic to extrinsic goals. [37] That is, placing more value of material awards and outside approval, over self-improvement or fulfillment.

However, despite research suggesting that there are those amongst us who have shifted focus, it's more of an exception to the rule, rather than the norm. Sure, who

[37] Ibid.

doesn't like a shiny new toy to play with, but not all of us are crows scavenging for bright objects to fill up a nest. Admittedly some of us may be drawn to the need to collect. Let's face it, the ribbons and trophies that we lined up on our walls and dressers growing up as kids, kind of set a precedent, right? However, there are those of us who aren't necessarily this way inclined—having either survived a relatively unscathed hands-on childhood, or over time, have naturally (or with the help of a therapist) been able to tap into the deeper values-based system that sits at the heart of us.

The rewards that we do get in material form, often bring with them a sense of fulfillment. Not because of what they are per se, but because of the very efforts and commitment that we've had to put in, to achieving the result. We work out arses off to achieve things—so when we do have something to put in our hot little hands, something concrete and tangible that we can sniff, taste and touch for our efforts—it makes the journey of getting there all the worth it.

A good news story would end here saying something along the lines of, 'All's well that ends well: Millennials break even with trophy in one hand and sense of fulfillment in the other.' However, this isn't quite the case—instead falling more appropriately under the category of what even Trump would consider 'fake news'. 'Fake' being the word of the day here, because the sense of fulfilment we expect to get out of whatever we achieve these days, isn't even remotely what it was once upon a time. The sense of fulfillment and satisfaction that ran through our little bodies in the past, when we reached the finish line of a race, or received a gold star on our test, wasn't just a feeling for us. It was a feeling shared by our parents and any other onlookers who happened to be there at the time. Sure, the 'winner' sign may have faded in colour and have been passed by hundreds of other kids already, but it didn't matter. In our minds, and in the minds of our parents, we were winners. The reward— whether it was a pizza dinner, ice-cream, movie treat, or late-night curfew being extended—brought us a sense of achievement because we'd earnt that privilege. It wasn't about crossing the line or getting the gold star: it was also about sharing in the afterglow of the effect. That warm feeling that lasted for weeks.

Now, we've all heard the saying, 'All good things must come to an end.' That seemingly wise idiom reminding us that nothing good lasts forever; arguably sucking the life out of any hope, dream or sense of long-term pleasure we think we might gain, from anything that happens to make us feel good. While a contentious discussion on its own—one which will be avoided for the sake of tangents—we can, in a similar fashion, apply the same adage to our generation. What has become apparent, is the fact that we millennials have spent so much time achieving goals and receiving rewards, that our satisfaction threshold has elevated so much so, we're barely hitting the mark anymore.

When we think about the reward feedback loop, it's easy to find examples. Think about sex or drugs: an instant reward, which we don't have to work hard for (well, in most cases), accompanied by a 'high' and satisfaction factor that also in itself, tends to be short lived. Conversely if we think about longer term pursuits, such as completing an exam, the notion of instant gratification is delayed until we reach the goal, and while working to get to that point, we're needing to put a heck of a lot of effort in. Therefore, our sense of achievement after finishing the exam, or receiving results, tends to hang around for more than a few hours (unlike post coital highs). So, based on this, one could logically assume that the longer we work toward a goal and the more time we invest, our feelings of satisfaction and fulfillment are also equally going to last a while.

However. This is not proving the case at all for millennials, as our feelings of fulfillment are passing by like an express train. The highs that we feel, irrespective of how much blood, sweat and tears we've put into something, are vanishing—as we quickly move on to the next thing. An endless pursuit of trying to find 'more' in extrinsic goals and motivation. We weren't taught as kids that our self-worth wasn't supposed to be measured by our achievements. even though it may feel that way. The reality is, our parents loved us for who we were (and are) and while the encouragement factor to achieve was an OTT epic fail, it wasn't to shape our generation into becoming materialistic. Not at all. It was done through goodwill and intention. The downside for us, is that the warm, bright feelings of accomplishment wear off faster every time we achieve something, leaving us feeling empty and in need to search again. Creating what has become a generation of desensitized individuals: us.

#Michelangelo's in the making: Perfectionism

Millennials suffer from a stronger perfectionist trait than other generations.[38] In fact, studies show that our generation feel overburdened with a perfectionist streak, which other generations haven't quite seen. Alarmingly, it's not just perfection in its 'simple form' that is affecting millennials. We are suffering from what's considered 'multidimensional perfectionism' (yes, there is such a thing), which can be broken down into three components.

First, we have our own, self-oriented perfectionism — which is basically an irrational need to reach overly ambitious goals. Second, there is socially prescribed perfectionism — the external pressure we feel from others to achieve. Third, we have the 'other-oriented' perfectionism — which is largely based on having unrealistic expectations of others. Or put simply, because we're all internal perfectionists, living in a perfectionist fuelled society, we expect others to be perfect. Which is, quite frankly, encouraging a world of superficiality: hello, Dorian Gray.

---

[38] Curran. T., and Andrew, P.H. (2019). Perfectionism Is Increasing Over Time: A Meta-Analysis of Birth Cohort Differences From 1989 to 2016. *Psychological Bulletin* 145(4), 410-429.

In looking at the millennial generation versus our parents or grandparents, the biggest rise that's been seen across perfectionism trends is external pressure perfectionism. Is this surprising? Absolutely not. The reasons, born out of the same old stories of competitiveness, a focus on individualism (or achievements), overbearing parents and social media.

#Success. You can't add water and stir

Alongside achievement, comes success. While the definition of success can be loosely described as the 'accomplishment of an aim or purpose', it's always going to be subjective. While some people have tried to quantify success,[39] (irrespective of this approach seeming rather absurd), if we look at our generation and what success means, we see a definition that is either not defined, or ridiculously skewed. Unfortunately, the world hasn't helped us. We've grown up during a time—and currently living in an era—where things are given to us much faster than previous generations. Think about it. We've microwave ovens, fast food restaurants, the internet,

---

[39] Malcolm Gladwell, author of *Outliers* (2008) states that it takes at least 10,000 hours of practice before a person becomes a success.

phones and same day services. Instant and immediate are the norm. Not to mention the media's saturation and bombardment of celebrities, TV personalities and actors that have become overnight successes. What this has done, is created a culture which have expectations that, along with a cup of instant coffee, success will be ready when we add boiling water and stir. The reality is, overnight sensations are not going to happen. Success isn't going to be delivered to your door on a silver platter courtesy of Amazon—unless we take that platter and fill it with a redefined notion of what success means to us. What we've failed to remember is that like most things, success is subjective. What you think or deem as success versus someone else, is going to be different. Success is defined by you. Which might simply be getting home before your flat mate, dominating the couch and binge-watching Breaking Bad.

#What do you mean not everything that pops into my head goes on social media? Isn't that what everyone does?

Our relationship with social media can be arguably summed up by the status: it's complicated. It's not surprising when you consider the dynamics of pairing a generation who were raised to be competitive and success-driven with a 'small world' connected through social media. Unlike previous generations who tended to have a little privacy with life events, we're the first generation to have gone through all the trials of reaching adulthood through the ever-present lens of social media—complicating what is an already challenging stage of life. Rather than transitioning from child, to teen, to adult, supported with what was, once upon a time age appropriate stimulus, we've been robbed of this. Instead, we've been confronted with the opinions and photos of every Tom, Dick and Harry, society breathing down our neck, in addition to our raging emotions and hormones. Which does not create an optimal environment for healthy development on any level—physically, emotionally or mentally. As life goes on, we are constantly made aware of the activities of everyone around us through social media. We are constantly hearing about what this person did that was amazing, or what that person has achieved—saturated by other people's achievements, accolades, titles, and awards. Placing us in a position where we start wondering, 'What am I doing?', 'What should I be doing?' or 'Is this enough?' Of course, we don't set out to intentionally or deliberately start comparing ourselves to others, or silently berate ourselves for not having achieved what someone else has—whether it be from a career, personal or life trajectory point of view. But when the messages we see each day are of this nature—the 'highlight reel' of everyone's life—it's hard not to wonder.

The truth is, we've all at times put on the self-criticism hat and mulled over our own lives when looking at the filtered version of someone else's. And while there's nothing *that* wrong about taking a reflective approach at times (we are human after all), the healthy self-reflection component has become lost on us, replaced by comparison. The problem of comparison has aggregated the anxiety that millennials are either already feeling, or about to, most likely in the form of social anxiety: a state of suffering caused by worrying about whether we're 'measuring up'. Which, by default, brings with it FOMO: fear of missing out syndrome (because let's be honest, even a night out can become a bragging point, or another way to prove an exciting life is being lived, right?).

But underneath all the glitz and glamour, we forget that the highlight reel is full of the shiniest parts of everyone else's lives, which never addresses the boring bits or failures. Think about it. When was the last time you saw a post being shared about supermarket errands, kids drop off, PTA meetings, cleaning the toilet, arguing with a partner, getting a speeding ticket, being fired or getting evicted? Or, photos of a unkept house, bank statements reflecting little funds, student debt invoice from the government, or a red faced and crying selfie? You probably haven't—or if so, very few. Why? Because these 'unglamorous' insights would taint the impression of us needing to live in an up-market rendition of *A Perfect Life*.

The payoff to all this superficiality, and falling part of the wave of BS, is that studies are increasingly showing how social media is impacting the mental health of millennials. Anxiety, stress and depression have been correlated with its use. And of course, the more social media platforms we use and the more time we spend on social media, the more at risk we become to experiencing these conditions. Which shouldn't come as any surprise. So, next time you're scrolling through the feed highlights remember the following: Confidence is silence. Insecurities are loud.

#I'll be happy when, exactly?

Compared to other generations, studies suggest that millennials are unhappier and lonelier. A happiness study which started in the 1970s (presumably warming up for our arrival), found an unusual trend in that people aren't becoming happier as they get older.[40] Fingers pointing to economic insecurity and the associated fears we all have about not being able to achieve what we expect. But not just our expectations, it's the expectations that others have of us. Yes, our parents and teachers have of course, during our early lives, given us resources, means and motivation to succeed—but at the cost of what have become for us, deep-rooted expectations to constantly achieve. We've never really been asked to do a stock-take on our expectations to see whether they're realistic. We've never been told to ask ourselves the question of whether the goals and pursuits we're pursuing are those that we want to be pursing, rather than those that are expected of us.

---

[40] Twenge, J. 2006. Generation Me: Why Today's Young Americans Are More Confident, Assertive, Entitled - and More Miserable Than Ever Before. Free Press, U.S.

When it comes to loneliness, millennials might as well be auditioning for a 2019 remake of the Akon classic, *Lonely*. Admittedly, the issue of loneliness is often hidden and less prominently discussed, most likely because we tend to attribute 'loneliness' with older people. But research is in fact showing that loneliness is greatest amongst teenagers and young adults.[41] Which presents an interesting conundrum given the plethora of ways we can connect with others or engage in activities.

When we talk about loneliness, it's important to be clear on what we're talking about. There's a difference between being or feeling lonely and being alone; the main difference being that we can be alone, and not feel lonely. If fact, ask most people, and there'll be some degree of want, or need, in being able to be alone, or have 'me time'. The loneliness aspect tends to become problematic when the loneliness we feel, starts to become a sense of isolation, or disconnect from others. Not just physically either. It's when we start to feel lonely even when we're surrounded by others.

---

[41] Holt-Lunstad, J., and Smith, T.B. 2016. Loneliness and social isolation as risk factors for CVD: implications for evidence-based patient care and scientific inquiry. *Heart* 102(13), 987-989.

Why should we care? Because if we don't tread carefully, loneliness can become yet another risk factor for our mental health. Studies have found that lonelier millennials are more likely (twice in fact) to experience mental health problems, such as anxiety and depression.[42] Lonely millennials are also more likely to disregard their physical health and engage in negative health behaviours like smoking and putting exercise on the back burner. Confidence is impacted, as is general outlook on life—so unemployment becomes common. And with all this, rather than reaching out for help, millennials are more likely going to withdraw from others or complain. It's not a pretty picture.

The reasons for our loneliness are varied. Some blame the curse of social media as it reduces our people skills and connections with others, while others see it enhancing our ability to remain connected. There are the problems with the world: millennials having entered an economy still recovering from the fallout of the GFC, low wage growth, decreased job security and rising house prices, all

---

[42] Matthews, T., Danese, A., Caspi, A., and Fisher, H.L. (2018). Lonely young adults in modern Britain: findings from an epidemiological cohort study. *Psychological Medicine* 49(2), 268-277.

throwing the challenge gauntlet at us. Even with the uncertainty that goes hand in hand with this, we're still expected to keep up with the fast-paced existence of life, while juggling what feels like a million balls at once. It's no wonder that some of us simply want to run and hide in a closet, the words 'retreat, retreat, retreat' echoing through our ears as if we're on a battlefield.

#Yes. I mean no. I mean yes. Actually . . . wait. I'm unsure

There's much debate to be had around the notion of being able to 'let go and let live', so to speak. And while in an ideal world, we'd be able to let down our hair, run through the streets, screaming 'Freedom!' at the top of our lungs, the reality is, we'd not get far. We'd recoil quickly—as if all wearing toddler wrist straps—into the arms of a world that doesn't often accommodate an environment where we can throw caution to wind. Why? Because of the heavy burden of uncertainty either weighing on our shoulders or shackling our ankles, reminding us that we're stuck in a world where stability, security and prediction have all but become extinct. Uncertainty is one of the biggest factors underpinning anxiety and stress in our generation. Uncertainty in pathways after study, uncertainty in the job market, uncertainty of housing, uncertainty of ever paying off debt, uncertainty about where the world is going and whether we're going to be able to keep up with what is an excessively, increasing, fast paced social media fuelled world. It's exhausting. While some of us may have mastered the art of being able to flow with the tides of change of the world, the reality is, there are far too many of us millennials out there suffering in this state of being, feeling a complete lack of control in not just our lives, but how to go about handling it.

Millennial Survival Techniques

When it comes to dealing with the current reality, we have two options. First, is we assemble a millennial army, revolt, take over the world and simply fix the abysmal state we are in. We can argue rightly that governments across the world haven't quite realised that the future is going to be staked on us. Think about it. We have an ageing population, social care budgets in many countries are being slashed rather than funded, and some countries are cutting migration which means less workers to help boost already pitiful economies. The burden of debt which has been accumulated post GFC and through generally poor economic decisions, will be passed onto us. We'll be accountable for either repaying trillions of dollars of debt or finding a miraculous solution to give us a clean slate (which doesn't involve giving away 'free' money or simply printing more. Nice try, Italy). The ageing population means retirement will rev up, and we'll be carrying the burden of our older generations to their graves, all while we receive less support. As it is now, our generation are already being faced with the possibility of never being able to retire as any form of pension or superannuation will be worth pittance in years to come. So, even without a crystal ball, we get the gist of where the world is going—leading us to feel we're in an incredibly justifiable position to rebel.

However. You and I both know that changes don't happen overnight and that protests, or the threat of revolting doesn't always work (it currently isn't for Brexit, clearly). Even if we did happen to pull this off, we're unlikely to make that much of a dent, given the absence of control we have over most of the aforementioned factors. So. This leaves us with option two: an arguably smarter, simpler and less anxiety and stress provoking situation (which, to be fair, we kind of need). We become our own experts through knowledge and awareness, and put our otherwise therapy investment pennies, back into ourselves, by ourselves.

This isn't about downplaying the magnitude of what millennials are dealing with—it's simply about making the best of what we've got. And when it comes to mental health—and what is a growing epidemic for us—we must take it seriously. Get the help and support you need, because it is at times, a jungle out there. We all know that.

#Don't succumb to pressure. Make your own decisions

Ok, so we've grown up in a world where making our own decisions has been photo bombed by our parents and society, and we've experienced feeling forced into a mould that feels as claustrophobic as an ice cube in a freezer. But you know what, we can't help what happened, we can't go back and rewrite yesterday's news, but what we can do is kick on with life holding full, free rein over ourselves. That is, we have power my friends, to do whatever we want. Sure, our pathways to date may have been heavily influenced by others. For some of you, you might be in a state of uncertainty, not knowing if you're Arthur or Martha, or what you want to do with life— overwhelmed by indecision and a plethora of choice. Sure, restrictions exist, but it doesn't mean we need to fall into the cracks of the pavement and be trodden on by society: squashed and silenced. In case you haven't realised, life is a wonderful journey of discovery and we are, despite the annoyances that the world is testing us with, in a land of opportunity. We can be, do or have anything we want. Which means that there is no such thing as conformity, there is no such thing as right or wrong, there is no such thing as black or white, there is no such thing as 'should' or 'have to', and there is no such thing as failure.

Right now, wherever you are in life, you can make your own decisions. And if you have no idea about what it is you want, then all the better. This is an opportune time, where you can quite literally unleash the beast within, go all crazy and find out what you like. Some of us (you know who you are) have been living a life distracted by everything else and failing to find time to stop, think or ask ourselves intentional questions about our lives. It's time to start asking yourself what is it that *you* really want.

Oh, and remember, the ongoing reel you're seeing on social media with its perfect bodies, perfect lives and constant emphasis of everyone achieving goals on display, is a façade. Don't be a sheep and fall into the trap of the 'false lives'. At the end of the day, we all shit the same shit, right?

#Give yourself permission to learn and grow. Find out what it is you want

Whoever developed the notion that before graduating school we must pick one thing that we're going to engage in on a five-day a week basis for the rest of our lives, was clearly the most boring, mundane, individual to have walked the earth. It's no different from telling a child which parent to pick to live with after a divorce, or who they love the most: anxiety and fear racing through the body, causing extreme distress and in some case trauma, at making the wrong decision. It's nonsensical and absurd. Not to mention the person who developed a timeline of life events which supposedly makes you a better and more accepted human, if you happen to have a well-defined career, a house, a hubby or wife and two kids, all under the age of 30. Puh-lease.

Yes, we are in a world where things are changing and at times it might feel impossible that we can exert any control. But it's not an excuse; certainly not from taking ownership over our lives. Life isn't about getting from point A to B. Life is full of journeys and pathways. Life doesn't start happening when we suddenly pay off our student debt. Or when we find the person of our dreams through a dating app. Life is now. Which means that if you're miserably unhappy or feeling way off kilter because of life, then start by making the decision to do something about it. Get to know what you like. Find a hobby, meet people, travel, write, quit your job, set up a business (although not necessarily in that order). Do, try and be many things. The world is your oyster.

We need to start making choices that help us, not hinder us. If you don't know how to make a choice, politely remind yourself that every day you're making a plethora of choices: what time to get out bed, what to eat, what to wear, what to listen to, what to read, who to text, who to call—you get the picture. We are decision making gurus, so start harnessing some of that power in making 'big people' decisions. And as author Chris Brogan wrote, 'If you're not on the right path, get off it.' Power of choice, peeps.

#Perfection doesn't exist. True story

The desire to be perfect is overrated. As we know, and have felt at times, it's a burden that sits heavily on our shoulders, yet at the same time tantalises us like we're chasing a rabbit. On and on and on we go, chasing the fluffy white tail, until we blindly fall down a hole and into a world of pain. The sad truth, however, is that in the eyes of the perfectionist, there will never, nor can ever be, any state of perfection. Because for a perfectionist, nothing is ever perfect. The relentless standards and ongoing quest for more, make it an impossible achievement.

The perfection trait that our generation is carrying, shouldn't come at a cost to our wellbeing. Sure, who doesn't want things to go exactly to plan, or look completely and utterly fabulous on occasion? But why bother striving for something that you and I both know will not make you feel fulfilled or happy? Certainly not for the sheer amount of time and effort that you'll be funnelling in for momentary satisfaction, before you start measuring yourself against the rest of the world again. The pursuit of perfection is a disguise for insecurity. It becomes a statement that 'I'm not good enough just as I am'. A story that at some point in our lives we've bought—likely on sale for 50 percent off, gift wrap included. The fact is, humans were never intended to be perfect. It's part of the definition of being human. Embrace the imperfection of being human. Stop killing yourself and recognise already that you are good enough, as you are. You're a millennial after all, with two and half billion other peeps batting behind you, cheering you on as you are.

#Switch off

It's become obvious that there are far too many of us out there who are connected to social media but disconnected with ourselves. While we can easily put our fingers in our ears, sing 'La la la, I can't hear you', ignoring the glaringly obvious fact that social media has a huge correlation with damaging our mental health, it's not the optimum choice. Let's be honest with ourselves. No one wants to suffer with prolonged discomfort and negative impacts to their mental health. At least, not by choice.

It all boils down to the following: now being aware of the impacts of social media on your mental health, there is greater onus on you, my friend, to not just manage and monitor the time you're spending online, but your mental and emotional responses. We, as a generation, need to become aware of the causative factors to poor mental health, especially the risks associated with social media use. Otherwise, too many of us will continue to live an 'unconscious life'. One not only hindered by external factors in the world, but completely controlled by. Don't be an ostrich and bury your head in the sand.[43]

#Stay connected with real life humans

Believe it or not, human contact and kinship help alleviate anxiety. While we are living in a fast-paced world that is largely shaped by the incessant need to be 'on' all the time, it's important that we take time to be with others. When we have social support, we are better off psychologically. We only need look at other cultures, or

---

[43] Ok, so the saying is a myth. Ostriches don't bury their heads in the sand to avoid danger. Not only would they be unable to breathe and therefore suffocate and die, but when you think about it logically, they don't have a reason to—not when they can run at 40 miles per hour. Having said that, you get the point of the metaphor.

our ancestors (even as far back as cavemen days) to see how important community and social support is. Feeling connected with others and being part of a community, is something we all need. When we lose a sense of belong, or community, we set ourselves up for feeling anxious, isolated and alone. Take the time to chillax more often with other people, especially at times when you may be feeling dreadful.

#Ride the wave of uncertainty

Uncertainty is always going to exist, it's a fact. However, this doesn't mean that we can't take control over the now. Sure, we don't know what the future will hold, or where the world is going, but we can choose to live our lives in an empowered meaningful way.

Now of course we can resist the uncertainty around us, making things a lot harder than they must be. But the fact of the matter is, this current reality we're in—uncertain or not—is the world. So, we need to accept the world as it is, right now, and in doing so, own our power, our worth and to step forward into the world full of confidence. Tapping into those fabulous traits and qualities that make us the resilient bunch of peeps that we are. We don't have a crystal ball, nor can we exert that much influence over the current state of affairs of the world. So why get our knickers in a twist over things we can't change?

Control what you can. You.

#Come out from under the rock

As a generation, we have grown up with increased attention on mental health issues. We talk about it, know people impacted by it, hear about it in the news and see it play out in books, TV shows and movies. While not quite pop culture in the traditional sense, the topic is contemporary—which means that support out there, is aplenty. The slackening of stigma around mental health is something we can take advantage of. We shouldn't be in a position today where we're vilifying our aversive emotions and fighting them. We don't need to try to bury feelings like anxiety and stress. While admittedly we are a generation who are hard on ourselves, we are in a prime position to be able to milk the benefits of a more inclusive society of people, where support is there if we need it. Sure, sometimes we just feel bad, and there's nothing wrong with that. But if you need help, reach out. You are not alone.

Mental health issues can affect anyone. Present the opportune conditions and presto! There sprout the seeds for a challenging journey ahead. We've all suffered times where we want to throw a tantrum, bang our head on our desk, give the middle finger to the world, or scream at the top of our lungs for everyone to fuck off. Stress and pressure happen. It's life. But the reality we can't avoid, or hide from, is that the world today is presenting a plethora of challenges for millennials that are impacting our mental health—to levels and degrees that haven't been seen before. We need to start thinking about the 'why' and being more conscious of how we are living our lives: our emotions, our reactions and the levels of BS we're letting get under our skin. It's up to all of us, to take responsibility for our wellbeing and where needed, make adjustments and changes with our life. Mental health challenges are not insurmountable and can be mitigated through awareness, education and a concerted effort to put ourselves first. Protect your wellbeing. You owe it to yourself.

#Bring on rainbows and unicorns

CHAPTER 6

No, I Don't Love You Long Time: Redefining the Workplace

─────────○─────────

If we millennials received a dollar for every time someone used the words 'lazy', 'self-entitled' and 'unfocused' to describe how we operate in the workplace, we'd be able to pay off all our debts, and then some. For whatever reason, we've had words and phrases cast upon us from predecessor generations; words and phrases that have been conjured up out of ignorance. With this misjudgement, comes a range of preconceived notions, expectations and ideals projected toward us—which to be perfectly frank, have no basis of truth. In other words, complete BS.

Yes, we're misunderstood, to say the least. Which kind of sucks for employers because by 2025, 75 percent of the workplace will be made up of yours truly.[44] Millennials are the next generation of leaders; the peeps that will be running the show. The fact that there still exists a huge lack of understanding for our generation and we're still cursed at, is problematic for everyone. Think about it. No one wants their organisation being led by a bunch of disgruntled millennials. It's a sure-fire way to bring about disaster.

But before getting into the nuts and bolts of how we operate in the workplace, it's useful to look at the backdrop—that being, the makeup of the organisations we are working for. We are at a time in history, where we now have up to five generations working together. Now in a perfect world, we'd all be able sit in a circle, hold hands, chant 'Om' and accept everybody for who they were, differences included. A land of unicorns and rainbows it would be. But the reality is, we don't live in that kind of world—and at this rate, very unlikely to. Not for lack of want of course (I mean, who doesn't like glitter), but more due to reality.

---

[44] Big demands and high expectations: The Deloitte Millennial Survey. Deloitte. 2014.

Consider the dynamics of the workplace: hundreds, if not thousands of employees are pulled together under the one roof, all with different ages, sexes, cultures, religion — not to mention values, beliefs, attitudes and behaviours. Naturally, the diversity pool is going to equate to a colourful mix of happenings. Whether we like it or not, there are going to be times of difficulty in our workplaces—which may or may not manifest in a multitude of ways. From full blown confrontations, to passive aggressive emails, to exclusions from meetings, to having your lunch eaten from the fridge (yes, it happens), there are going to be challenging times for each of us. For millennials, we're likely going to feel these challenges in several ways; irritation being the understated commonality between them all. From difficult conversations with managers, to feeling excessively frustrated at not being where we want to be, to feeling pissed off that we're not being listened to, or had our needs met. Not that we have huge needs, just enough to cause discontent when we realise they aren't being fulfilled, or we're being made the mickey of. For example, just because we have an opinion doesn't mean we appreciate finding ourselves coming up against resistance, a solid brick wall or having 'Denied' stamped across our forehead. Or, discovering that being on an internship or having recently graduated means we're exceptional coffee makers, admin do-ers, errand runners or should be nominated for the first pub round. No, we've a little more substance than that.

We've all had situations in our careers where we've felt a disconnect between us, the job, the workplace, or all three. We've all been left scratching our heads, mulling over the words, 'What the fuck?', or thinking about quitting. We've all felt the bind of the 'one foot in, one foot out' approach to our jobs—not quite sure if it's for us, waiting patiently for it to improve, but equally not fully committing until we're sure (if that's even possible). It's a drain. And I'm not just talking about the emotional and psychological impacts on us, but literally to the workplace. Having unhappy or disconnected millennial employees is not where an organisation wants to find themselves. Not least because it's a pure waste of potential, talent and brainpower, but the 'keeping an eye on the periphery' thing we do, will have us eventually finding greener pasture, and like a heard of starved cattle, we'll stampede toward it.

So why do we come up against so much difficulty when all we want to do is find a job that we enjoy? A job that will provide us with opportunity, that we can balance with our lives and where we feel like we're making a difference to the world? Because we're working with a bunch of dynamics that if we don't know exist, can't play the workplace game in our favour.

#Say what, exactly?

Millennial issues aside for a moment, let's get back to workplaces in general. Have you ever stopped to think about the dynamics of workplaces and how—subtly or not—more broader issues play out? Let me give you an example:

'You need to prove yourself', were the words that rolled out of the mouth of my at-the-time Gen X manager, after I raised what I felt was a discrepancy with my level of output and work performance versus my salary. Now of course, the word 'No' isn't something any millennial likes to hear but coupled with an inference that my capabilities hadn't been noticed, or 'yet to be realised', felt like a kick in the teeth.

Perplexed and at a loss that my over-and-beyond-high-level-work-performance ethic, typical of our tribe wasn't enough, I asked for a 'please explain'. What eventuated, other than feeling incredibly pissed off at receiving a below par response which was centred around not having worked in the organisation long enough and not having had enough experience, was the realisation that this wasn't a dig at me. Yes, hard to believe, but in fact, true. Adopting the lens of 'let's be adults here', I realised that this was a fundamental generational issue, rooted in unconscious bias.

Resonate?

Let me explain. The reality is, each one of us carry bias. But not just bias per se, unconscious bias: the bias we don't know we have and are projecting at other people, until we're called out on it (note, like now). In the workplace, this can often manifest as intergenerational conflict—in a nutshell, that not-so-wonderful tension and friction that happens from exchanges between colleagues of different ages (or generations). These expectations or biases are founded or based upon our own individual experiences within our own generation. Because of our own experiences, we may be prone to labelling or attaching expectation or assumption toward the behaviour of another. Think about it for a minute. I'm sure you're guilty of having thoughts that older colleagues at some point, have either been too slow at doing something, too tech illiterate, or too regimented with their work schedule.

Case in point with the above. My then manager had beliefs about what I 'should be doing', based on Gen X experience, attitude and values. So, for me to 'prove myself' I'd need to follow a path based on her experiences and expectations— which would involve long term 24/7 commitment to the job, the organisation and a let's-be-patient approach until I'd seemingly served enough time in that position.

Kind of goes against our grains, right?

However, the good news story is that there is a way to mitigate the challenges. We just need to get real about two key things. The first, is what kind of people we are in the workplace. Basically, what we want, where our values are, what's going to get under our skin. The second, is being aware of where the pain points are going to be in the office with our colleagues—which means greater ability to put on our big boots and deal with things in a mature way.

Of course, after owning the situation, putting on my red 'Dorothy' shoes and clicking my heels, I found another job with an organisation who shared my values.

#Why we are the way we are

As the age old saying goes, 'You don't know, what you don't know.' So, if we don't understand what type of people we are in the workplace, then we run the risk of remaining in jobs we don't like or following suit to the rest of the cards in a very boring deck. Not to mention struggling with feeling disconnected.

So, what's our jam?

Non committed: We don't do workplace commitment like other generations did once before. We enter workplaces with a no-strings attached approach. We like flexibility and variety—and incredibly conscious that if an organisation can't meet our needs or values, then we'll politely leave. True story.

Short term focus: We aren't focused on the long term. Yes, we have goals and vision, but the reality is, we are open and accepting of change in our careers, especially if it gives us what we want.

Adaptable: Thanks to the levels of change and transition we've endured as humans, this has translated into us being highly adaptable and flexible employees, with an ability to multitask. This means that we like work that comes with variety and tend to get bored with 'same same' or routine.

Hardworking: We are hardworking, productive and motivated to achieve. Which means, thanks to our 'everyone gets a trophy' upbringing, when we're given a goal, we'll make it happen. However, our engagement will drop off if we're overburdened and have no time for personal life. Too big a workload is one of the top reasons we'll leave a job.

Tech Savvy: We use technology to get things done faster. Which means that our level of work effort is going to exceed what organisations once considered the average, because we're bringing the bread and butter of our native tech selves into the workplace. The only downside is when we find ourselves working for organisations where we feel like we've done a reverse *Hot Tub Time Machine* and gone back to the 80s — our natural state of getting things done pronto with technology being mis-matched with sluggish systems, or out-dated technology. Further to note, is that our preference for communication at work is also built around technology—think workplace IM chat.

Creative: We love to have creative freedom. We are innovative, think outside-the-box and offer fresh perspective and ideas. Think focus groups, workshops, collaboration. Give us a blank canvas and a pack of colourful markers and watch us make shit happen.

Purpose: Passion and purpose fall into our blood. Because we value the work we do, we want a workplace who equally values us and our efforts. Which means, we do want a thanks or a pat on the back every so often (and there's nothing wrong with that).

Opportunity: We have a want for learning, for discovery and opportunity. If we think something is going to make us more skilled, offer something of value or simply make us better people, we'll put our hands up. We also value and want those in our workplace to offer active feedback, encouragement and support—because we want to ensure that we're completing things the best way we can. We are also open to mentors. Yes, the residual high achiever and perfectionist traits play to this; but overall, we just want to make sure we're not wasting our time on the wrong path.

Autonomy: We want autonomy, not micro-management. We loathe politics and getting caught up in the red tape. We crave autonomy over what we do, when we do it, how we do it and who we do it with. Which is why we value—and seek out—flexible workplaces, and equally, leave workplaces which are too regimented.

Equals: We aren't attached to prestige or positions of authority. We want meaning and fulfilment in what we do, not necessarily an executive office. Well, maybe we all wouldn't turn down an office with skyline views of course, but the reality is, we're 'people' people and prefer to work as a team, rather than part of a hierarchical structure. We see everyone as equals, irrespective of job title.

Money: While we're not typically money motivated or seek jobs that just pay the big bucks, we are conscious that money matters. With the concerns we have about finances in general, especially about debt and paying our bills, we do place some emphasis on ensuring that we are compensated for our time and effort. Which doesn't mean we're snobs—we simply know what the market is offering from a salary perspective and want to make sure it matches up.

Fun: Our sense of community and work matters—which means we want work friends and a team that we feel comfortable being in every day. This also includes having a good manager—someone who shows interest and can connect with us.

It's an impressive list, right? Understanding our workplace values from a wider millennial perspective is key to ensuring that we are working in jobs and organisations that fit who we are—and if not, feel empowered to seek alternative pathways that will align with our values.

#Get to know your colleagues

When we look at the workplace, it's easy to see why, and where, pain points are going exist. Five generations working together means that people are going to ride on your nerves—and equally, you on theirs. Not from an intentional point of view (unless you're that way inclined) but the simple fact is, that just like our personalities, our working preferences are going to be different. From technology through to hierarchy. A critical factor that is often overlooked, is that when one generation replaces another in the work environment— for example, the rise in millennials and the retirement of Traditionalists and baby boomers—the overall environment becomes something new altogether, fundamentally changing staff morale, mood and behaviour. Which is why it's typically those organisations that are open and flexible to accommodating emerging employee demographics and trends, that we are drawn to. None of us want to work for an organisation whose practices or policy are Empire era-ish.

So where are we going to see fisticuffs happen in the office, other than over the free lunch?

When it comes to understanding authority:[45] Generations look at authority differently. Older generations see organisations and teams operating in a hierarchical environment. For older colleagues, formal authority and accountability are linked directly to

---

[45] Key areas of difference are cited in the following papers: *How Generational Differences Impact Organizations & Teams*. Birkman International. 2008; Tolbize, A. 2008. *Generational differences in the workplace*. Research and Training Center on Community Living. University of Minnesota, U.S.

hierarchy. This means there is a pecking order—formal lines of management and an expected obligation to show respect and courtesy to said structure. We millennials, however, tend to see things from an equal level. We consider competence and expertise as defining the formal authority structure—not someone's title or position (which is why calling your boss 'Mate', 'Bro' or 'Cous' isn't going to sit well). It can be a recipe for conflict and is a problematic area for workplaces because it gets misinterpreted constantly as either lack of respect, defiant behaviour or a sense of entitlement. Yes, we've all heard the criticism toward us. The same typically applies to supervision and management styles and the varying degrees to which generations appreciate supervision and feedback. We want feedback and value having a mentor, while older generations may be insulted by it.

When it comes to communication: Lack of communication or miscommunication is at the root of most issues. But it isn't just about what has or hasn't been said that is the cause of tension, but how people choose to communicate. How we choose to communicate is going to have an impact on the message we want to deliver, including how it's perceived. As a generation having grown up in a world of technology, having a conversation online or sending someone a short text to ask for something, is the norm. However, it isn't the norm for older generations—who tend to prefer you get up off your chair, walk over and engage in a face-to-face conversation—because sending a reply to your email or text is considered a burden. Not to mention impersonal.

The other issue with communication ties in with the below point on technology. While we may be adept with online social networking, we are falling short at times when it comes to 'real life' relationships. Some organisations rely very much on interpersonal relationships and connections to get things done or get them done efficiently. A point of contention for organisations especially when taking on 'younger' generations, is that we (and our Gen Z friends) have been observed to have a habit of holding back from reaching out to others or not knowing how to get information. The issue over whether technology is reducing our soft skills—particularly for the younger millennials—isn't new. We need to be conscious of the fact that our preference isn't always the most beneficial way of engaging with people.

When it comes to technology: Gone are the days of the pigeon carrier. The rapid rate of technology growth has changed the way we communicate, including speed, delivery and method. Older generations haven't grown up in the tech world like us, so naturally have taken time to develop confidence and trust. For older colleagues, value is placed in having built their own networks and forming connections via their bread and butter face-to-face meeting way. They value creating more personal and meaningful social engagement and experiences. The introduction of technology has had to take as a 'softy softy' approach – even if it has introduced a new and improved way of communicating. For millennials, the key is being mindful that just because we like it this way, others may not. Courtesy and respect go a long way when it comes to communication and you're better off creating conducive, productive relationships with colleagues, rather than creating enemies.

When it comes to change: Let's be honest. As resilient as we might feel when it comes to change, most people don't respond well. Think about the basics in the office, like smarter working systems and hot desking. Changes that we might see in practice as being refreshing, yet for other people has created stress, grief and on occasion, union involvement. While on face value people may appear to be adaptable to change, resistance in one way or another is likely to exist. As millennials are a little more flexible in the approach to workplaces, it can cause friction with others because it's not familiar and therefore equates to a bad thing. Of course, we know it isn't; but having more respect and tolerance for other colleagues who may like their Monday morning routine, 10:30 a.m. on-the-dot coffee or fixed desk position, can go a long way.

When it comes to performance and productivity: The perceived decline in work ethic across the generations is a contentious topic. Yes, we all know that millennials are tarnished with the lazy-and-don't-know-what-work-is brush. But the reality is, evidence doesn't support the claim that there is a decline in work ethic among us. In fact, it's the opposite. Great news for us, but not so much so when the translation hasn't happened, or we have our colleagues Chinese-whispering around the office that we're lazy. The fact is, it's merely a perception rather than reality. Older generations believe that a strong work ethic is demonstrated by being part of the organisation—being physically present at the office for hours on end. Now, while doing face time in the office might translate to 'working', research has demonstrated the contrary with how time is spent in the office (i.e. the actual time working). The eight-hour standard workday isn't based on the optimal number of hours a person spends concentrating on work. In fact, if you're working in the U.K. (no disrespect to our British friends) studies have shown that during an eight-hour day, only two hours and twenty-three minutes (or a quarter of the time) is spent being productive.[46] So, while your boss might be requesting you do face time and be in the office, the fact is, it doesn't translate into productivity. We've already picked up on this trend—which is why we want our work to be judged on its merits, not the amount of time we spend in the office. Hence the reason why we're happy to adopt a flexible working approach to both work location and the hours we work.

---

[46] *How Many Productive Hours in a Work Day? Just 2 Hours, 23 Minutes.* Vouchercloud. 2018. https://www.vouchercloud.com. Of the 1,989 U.K. office workers surveyed, only twenty-one percent believed they were productive the entire day. Seventy-nine percent were open enough to admit they weren't productive at all! Kudos to honesty. The biggest time waster? Checking social media (47 percent). No surprise.

#Still feeling the pinch

It wouldn't be millennial to sit and blow our own trumpet, so with that in mind, we need to accept that there are a few other grievances, so to speak, about us that have been observed. They aren't what would be considered deal breakers to employing us but are enough of an issue to get under the skin of our colleagues.

Showing initiative: This criticism tends to relate to new graduates who appear to struggle in transitioning to a working environment where they need to show initiative to ensure their time is used productively, especially if they encounter problems. Some have been reported to expect managers or colleagues to solve their problems instead of using initiative and resourcefulness to overcome obstacles. Now, while we could easily blame it as an offset of helicopter parenting and technology, it would be foolish to not take responsibility. For those of you who've been that person, or are currently that person, ask for help. Reach out to managers or find a colleague who can provide some mentoring. You don't want to develop a reputation for being 'that person'.

Making decisions: We all know that being presented with too many options isn't a good thing. The overwhelm we've felt at times in our personal life when faced with a smorgasbord of options is also contagious in the workplace. We have been criticised for not being able to make decisions. Our managers and colleagues simply want us to make an educated choice; not sit in agony and take an age to make up our mind (even if all solutions presented appear as good as one another). We all know this stems from our need-to-get-it-right perfectionism traits—but the downside is, spending time researching something to death and still not deciding, brings about anxiety. We've all heard the saying, 'Fake it until you make it'. There is a lot to be said in confidence. So, make a decision and own it. Be confident in yourself.

Expectations on career progression: This is a big one: the mismatch of expectations, most commonly seen between new employees (or graduates) and existing staff. Admittedly, we have all been guilty at times, of bringing an unshakeable sense of self-belief and entitlement attitude to the office—despite having only just set off on our career. While our level of self-assurance is commendable, it's unfortunately made us look arrogant to our peers. Instant gratification victims or not, we need to be mindful of being able to separate the pressing need for 'now' when it comes to our work or careers. Yes, have a level of drive, have desire to be a leader, to manage, to climb whatever corporate ladder you want—but be mindful that you're not going to cover five years' experience in six months within a company. We need to consider the wider dynamics at play too—such as older colleagues who have had to form their careers based on values such as years of service. It's not to say you won't end up moving through the company at pace, but in the meantime exercise a little patience and respect that not everyone sees the workplace like we do.

Millennial Survival Techniques

Whether you love or loathe the job you're currently in, there's never been time like the present to ask yourself the following: 'What the hell am I doing?' Ok, so maybe tone it down a notch to a more level-headed: 'Do I feel fulfilled?' If the answer is 'No', then you need to be asking 'Why?' Is it because you've ended up in career that you didn't want? Is it because you're feeling misunderstood in the workplace and suffering from intergenerational tensions? Is it because you're a commitment-phobe and twelve months in, you're ready to call 'no deal' and make a dash? Is it simply because you've no fucking idea what you want to do and the job you are in isn't putting the butter on your bread (or for you gluten free peeps, the rice in your sushi roll)? Regardless of the answer, the most important thing is to ask yourself the question: Why?

For those of us feeling the pinch of conventional workplaces, or subtle tension in the office amongst colleagues, there are things we can do to mitigate our want to suddenly quit.

#Deal with difficult people like a pro

Keeping your millennial head high, remaining unoffended and not taking things personally following less than ideal workplace conversations, isn't always going to be easy. In fact, it's going to grate on your nerves and get under your skin more than you realise. Until you decide to look at it through a different lens. The lens of: it's not you, it's me (or, it is you, but I'm being polite about it).

Identification: Identify the issue. Intergenerational differences are real (and normal). We are all biased. We all have different values. Get over it.

Understanding: Understand that the situation, or conversation, isn't personal. Sure, it might feel personal, but when you remove your bruised ego, it will help you gain much needed clarity.

Communication: Communicate respectfully and authentically. Acknowledge that the reason the person has said what they have or behaved in a certain way is rooted in their own workplace values—which are not going to be the same as yours. Or they might just be having a shit day. It happens.

Acceptance: Accept the differences between perspectives, values and beliefs. We are all different. When we understand and respect other people and their values, then we can interact in a more effective manner. Put up the white flag and take the time to walk in the shoes of your colleagues.

Gratification: Finally, express gratitude for whatever outcome transpires. Yes, it might be hard if you're suddenly sacked, but if that's the case then the job wasn't for you anyway. When one door closes, another will open. It always does.

#Find a supportive manager

It's no secret that employee engagement is a challenge at the best of times for organisations—and that's putting aside the shared Monday morning office vibe of sheer disappointment. However, the effort invested in addressing employee engagement is often well below par of where it could be. It shouldn't come as a surprise, especially to us millennials, because we know what it's like when we don't feel there's reciprocal investment happening from our organisation. We start to become disengaged, and in some cases bored. And alarmingly, there is a growing percentage of us who are feeling unsupported and dissatisfied—which means shitty times all round. The key to helping us achieve what we want and moving from a 'Can't be arsed' state to a 'Let's make it happen' state, is finding great managers. People who can help us harbour our goals, help fulfil our 'why', improve our professional lives and make us feel supported and understood. Finding a good manager, or mentor, may make all the difference in shifting where you are right now, to where you want to be.

#If it's not for you, then move on

There's no point staying in a job or career that isn't making you happy. It might sound easier said than done, but it's not. The upper hand we have when it comes to the workplace (and life) is we've enough confidence in ourselves to value our worth. Not from a 'the world owes me' perspective, but an acceptance that if a job doesn't gel, we have enough courage to find something else. It's within each of us. We are always going to be subjected to societal pressures and pre-defined ways of living, being or doing. The challenge we face is becoming friends with the courageous part of ourselves. Or quite frankly, having enough balls to change our situation. We all have free will and we all have choice. Making conscious decisions in the best interests of us, of our livelihood and our future, is the smartest thing we can do. Not just for us, but for the rest of our millennial tribe who at some point, look to other millennial role models for guidance and courage. That person, may in fact, be you.

Be a millennial you'd be proud of.

#Be your own boss

CHAPTER 7

Can I Really Be Me? Breaking Free from the Chains of Society

―――――○―――――

Social expectations: *general standards of behaviour that individuals who live within a society are expected to uphold.*

Social norms: *unwritten rules about how to behave; accepted standards of behaviour.*

Conformity: *behaviour which fulfils social norms.*

Millennials: *failing apparently, at all the above.*

Ever found yourself asking the question, 'What happened to the simple life?' The life when we were younger, when we were kids. When responsibilities, stress and pressure didn't exist. When money didn't matter. When our career or job wasn't important. When marriage, kids and owning a home were things that happened in movies. Things that adults did. Things that we didn't have to worry about because they might happen 'one day'; a future so far away it was never even considered.

Then out of the blue, 'one day' suddenly shows up. Laden with all the experiences and teachings given to us over the years. Expectations. Pressures to conform. Pressures to achieve. To succeed. And we find ourselves in a state of being where we're so wired, we can't switch off. Brains in overdrive. Anxiety levels rising. Irritability sitting in the seat of our pants like hot coals. We feel behind in where we are 'supposed to be' in life, we've not lived up to our parents' expectations, we fear if we take time off work we'll be sacked, and if we don't get the top degree then we've got thousands of dollars' worth of debt, all for nothing. We're all trying to achieve that 'perfect life', constantly striving for achievements and success, because it's what we're being encouraged to do. But the downside is, it eventually becomes too much for us to cope with, leaving us feeling mentally, physically and emotionally violated—not to mention morbidly incapable of continuing to play what's become an unfair game. All of this leaving us wanting to scream at the top of our lungs, 'What the fuck happened?' or causing that 'seemingly unrelated' random 5 a.m. drunk-in-the-gutter-and-having-a-meltdown moment.

Life can feel bloody hard.

But have you ever stopped to question it? Stopped to think about whether the life you are currently living is in line with *your* ideals. As in fuck-everyone-else-I-couldn't-give-a-rats-ass-because-this-is-my-life, way?

Probably not.

Why? Well, the world doesn't make it all that easy. Let me explain.

If you thought being mollycoddled by your parents was enough, think again. Like a game of 'tag', parental overkill gets a swap for society. Who don't, I must add, give us anywhere near the same amount of nurturing and support as our dear parents (even if OTT). More commonly, when society steps up to the plate, it brings its A Game: a shit ton of bricks. Now, as to be expected, society harbours a range of beliefs and values that on a collective level are shared. Think to the above points: social expectations, social norms, conformity. Now while on the surface there seems to be nothing untoward about this, the reality is the impact it's having is profound.

Think about the world we live in. Each day we're bombarded with messages from the rest of the world. What to wear, what programs on Netflix to watch, what opinion to have. To get a job, be educated, fall in love. How many times have you picked up a newspaper or magazine and read article after article about the ideal life of someone else? The 'ideal' life that often involves overnight success or fame, a drop-dead gorgeous husband or wife, a Wills and Kate happily ever after, two adorable children who resemble cherubs, bucket loads of money, cars for all seasons and enough properties to consume a Monopoly board. How many times have you watched a movie where the 'ideal' life is hammered to death by the same message? Must do this. Must have this. Must take this life course.

Almost the entirety of our social world is built upon agreed constructs and messages. Why? So, we can function and communicate with others in what's considered a constructive manner. And while societies may differ across the world when it comes to norms or expectations, they all have one thing in common: they govern the norm. And like goldfish swimming around a confined bowl, we often don't take time reflect. Rather we think we're doing well, operating in our day to day lives like everyone else. That is, until we lose perspective and hit the glass bowl surface, hard, head on. Or when we notice the floating shadow above our head is our mate Barry, who's now dead; waiting to be scooped out and flushed down the toilet. All before he even had a chance to discover that his routine of eating the same fish food, at the same time each day and swimming umpteen circles were in fact imposed, rather than chosen. Or discovering that there are in fact, plenty of fish in the sea, and his life would have gone on post the short-lived love affair with Wanda. If only he had taken a leap of faith.

Now of course we're not goldfish, we're human. But the sad fact is, there's a lot of us millennials out there living goldish lives in a self-imposed tiny world, where we either feel there's nothing outside of the ins and outs of each and every day (or, 'the norm'), or we can't make our own choices. Why? Because our beloved society is constantly sending out messages, judgments, perceptions, expectations and pressures. All of which we have a ghastly habit of conforming to, like we're sheep.

#Who said we have to give a shit about 'the norm'?

We've all heard it. Millennials are 'stunted', 'immature' and 'failing at life' because we don't own homes, marry and have children before the age of 30. We're the subject of headlines such as, *Why Don't Millennials Grow Up* or *Millennials: A Generation Who Can't Get Their Shit Together*, copping criticism and flack for not conforming to what society—or more specifically, sociologists—have deemed as milestones that apparently make us 'adults'. These milestones have also fallen part of general social expectations and norms for centuries (give or take) and include finishing school, moving out of home, becoming financially independent, getting married and having children. Milestones that were developed in what seems like an age ago and haven't quite caught up on the same band wagon as the concept of change—placing us in a position where the world is changing rapidly, yet we're still expected to operate and behave in outdated, traditional ways. No wonder we're feeling confused; being pulled from pillar to post on what we're supposed to be doing versus the absence of a conducive environment that allows us to make that happen.

In fact, there is a period of our lives which has been classified to represent the span between adolescence and adulthood.[47] According to psychologists, it's the period of our lives where we typically become more independent and explore various life possibilities, usually between 18 and 25 years. Now the point of the theory is that first, it's a new demographic: that being, it's not something that our parents would have heard of, or identified with, because unlike our generation who at these ages don't have kids, live in our own homes or have enough money to become fully independent, our parents, and even our grandparents, would have had that. Second, that the theory itself is also contentiously changing, thanks to it being highly controversial within the developmental field, with psychologists arguing over its legitimacy. Which is mostly over the identity component that comes with the theory—namely that these years also mark a period of our lives where we're trying to work out who we are and forming an identity: that age-old question of: Who am I? Agreement or not, one could argue that it's

---

[47] Arnett, J. J. (2000). Emerging adulthood: A theory of development from the late teens through the twenties. *American Psychologist* 55(5), 469-480.

not quite the optimum period to be making big decisions, right?

According to the U.S. Bureau of Statistics,[48] if we were living in the 1960s then it would be reasonable to expect that about 65 percent of women and men would have passed these milestones by age 30. Think about our parents. In comparison to you and I, they probably appear to have had their shit together back then. Come the turn of the century with the year 2000, it was reported that only 50 percent of women and 33 percent of men reached those milestones. If we were to take a stab at the current rate for our generation, it would well and truly make yet another headline story for the rest of the world to point at. Having said that, this delay is legit. In fact, studies are supporting that the general transition into adulthood has shifted across the generations.[49] Most significantly pointing out the age equivalent milestone is 30:25. That being, age 30 has become the new point at which we tick all these boxes, rather than the once upon

---

[48] Henig, R. H. What is it about 20-somethings? *New York Times*. 2010.
[49] Carnevale, A.P., Hanson, A.R., and Gulish, A. 2013. *Failure to Launch: Structural Shift and the New Lost Generation*. Georgetown University Center on Education and the Workforce. U.S.; *Delayed transitions of young adults*. Statistics Canada. Government of Canada. 2014. https://www.statcan.gc.ca

a time 25-year-old. The good news is by doing so, we're shaking up the status quo of the world and bringing our own timelines. Boo yeah. The bad news? It's not something we can change or control because it's dependent on world climate and trends. In some cases, it might have given us the perfect excuse to roll over and play dead or fob it off as an issue that the world can deal with, but the reality is, we're suffering. Mostly from pressure—including pressure that everyone else is forcing upon us.

Considering the context of our young adult years, it doesn't take a rocket scientist to work out that there are practicalities in the choices we are now making. Shacking up with our parents for longer, staying single and being conscious of both our money and time, are decisions that we're having to make; not so much out of preference (even if our values are different), but because we're not stupid. To recap and offer some perspective for those of you who are feeling the dynamic pressures of society: the cost of college has tripled from 1980 to 2011 and our median wages have dropped 6 percent from 2007 to

2011.[50] In fact, the average age at which we are reaching the median wage increased between 1980 and 2012 from 26 to 30 years.[51] Factor in this slothful wage growth with the rising cost of living and study debt—which is typically US$35,000[52]—and we find ourselves pinching our arses at the merr thought of any other cash outlay. Which is why we've become rational beings in the choices that we make where money is an issue. Think marriage and kids. Decisions that we're postponing because of the bad economy and lack of financial security we have (thank you, GFC).[53] And when you consider how much it costs to raise a child from birth through age 17—what studies report to be a hefty US$233,610, excluding college fees – it make sense to heed caution.[54] If we are struggling to pay down our US$35,000 in student loan debt on a ten-year repayment plan, how on earth are we going to

---

[50]Fry, R. 2012. Young, Underemployed and Optimistic. Coming of Age, Slowly, in a Tough Economy. Pew Research Centre, U.S.

[51] Ibid.

[52] Sparshoot, J. Congratulations, Class of 2015. You're the Most Indebted Ever (For Now). *The Wall Street Journal*. 2015.

[53] Ibid.

[54] Lino, M., Kuczynski, K., Rodriguez, N., and Schap, T. 2017. *Expenditures on Children by Families, 2015*. U.S. Department of Agriculture.

handle an extra US$250,000 over the course of 17 years on top of that?

But then it's not just the financial cost per se, there's also an opportunity cost that comes with having a child: our career. While it does impact mums and dad alike, typically it's women who are impacted the most, particularly by having children in their 20s. Studies have found that women between ages 40-45 with professional degrees and full-time jobs who gave birth to their first child at age 35, made US$50,000 more per year than women who had their first child at 20.[55] Yep, kind of a big deal. But alas, that's not all. Think of it from a strategic perspective. If we're waiting to have children until our mid-30s, then we're well into an established career—which means our reputation and professional experience could easily be leveraged for greater flexibility and more family-friendly benefits.

See the problem is, when the world judges us millennials for not having ticked off everything in our twenties, they fail to take these factors into consideration.

---

[55] Martin, J.A., Hamilton, B.E., Osterman, M.J.K., et al. (2015). Births: Final data for 2013. *National Vital Statistics Reports* (67)(1), 1-69.

The other side of the coin to the milestone dilemma, is the fact that we're not cut from the same mould as the seeming Victorian Era, half the world is still living in. No, no, no. We're a new breed of peeps who know we have choice. Choice that is fuelled by the simple fact that we've discovered that the world is a playground, oozing with more opportunity than we can poke a stick at—multiple times. We have an amazing ability to see opportunity and potential in just about everything. We only need to look around the world to see what our generation has created, built upon, leveraged off, or exploited. The jackpot of opportunity that we have—irrespective of the economic issues that have practically jumped into bed with us—are right in front of us. Well, maybe slightly to the left and a little concealed, but still there.

Because of the opportunity factor that gently beckons to us, caressing us like a seductive Fabio French lover, we find ourselves opening like an Anne Geddes baby, blossoming out of a tulip. The more we come to realise that the world isn't a 4x4 sandpit, but rather an endless field, we can't help but want to jump in like excited children and try things out. It's not to say that we can't embark on wonderful new adventures with a mortgage, marriage and kids. However, it's going to be a heck of a lot easier to experience said adventures more freely, without worrying about getting whiplash when the commitment leash yanks you back.

And when all things considered—like the state of the world today—we're not going to rush into making huge commitments and bite off more than we can feasibly chew in our taco-filled-downed-by-craft-beer mouths, now are we? It's called making practical, rationale, mature decisions. Not quite the fools people think we are, huh?

The reality is, we come to this world with a different value system. What we want, what we value and where we find fulfilment, isn't the same as other generations. We want to live life. Like, live it: in the bold-underlined-highlighted-72-font-capital-letters way. For us, finding meaning and happiness in our life doesn't—nor shouldn't— depend upon, or be measured against what society has set as a benchmark. Sure, there are plenty of us out there who may have ticked off these things or working toward them, and that's ok. But if that's the case, then the 'when' these get achieved isn't a reflection of us failing. It doesn't mean we're falling behind, or any less of an adult because we decided that right now isn't the optimum time for us. Then there are some of us that frankly feel these milestones don't work at all. We might feel that the concept of marriage is flawed or that we'd prefer to invest our money into travel or the side gig we have, as opposed to taking out a home loan.

But with all that said, the fact is, we unfortunately don't often see the conundrum we are in: We are judged for not having ticked off key milestones; yet can't feasibly achieve these given the world climate. We are judged for having a different opinion and making decisions that go against the grain of the norm; yet we are born with different values and wants that inherently don't fit. We are pushed to justify our decisions and explain our reasonings; yet have never turned around to society and said, 'Hang on, what about your decisions?' It's like trying to fit a square peg into a round hole. And on, and on, and on, it goes until like all things, someone gets injured. That being, us.

Millennial Survival Techniques

There's something comforting knowing there are two and a half billion millennials out there in the world who are on the same wavelength. Sure, we might not speak the same language, live in the same parts of the world, or share culture, but underneath it all, we're peeps who've all grown up in the same era, facing the same issues, challenges and perks. Those very things outlined in this book—the big topics of discussion—they my friends, are what we all face together. And while we're not out there high fiving every person who looks like they were born between 1980 and 2000 or feel cause to become mates with those people who look or behave like us, there is an underlying shared sense of the world, uniquely seen through our eyes.

While not wanting to turn this final chapter into a tale of millennial group hand holding, swaying to the rhythm of 'Om' chanting or Mariah Carey's *We belong together*, it should be acknowledged that if anyone is going to understand where we're coming from, or who we are at the core, it's going to be each other. Which, I must say, is quite the benefit.

It goes without saying that we are, and quite possibly will always be, the most misunderstood generation. Subject to misconceptions, stereotypes and labels that we could start collating into a *101 Terms for Millennials* glossary that we could mass distribute to the world as a tongue-in-cheek gesture, sit back quietly and laugh at the absurdity of how it all came to be. All while putting proceeds of sale into our back pocket as compensation and a bit of 'up yours' for the world's ignorance and judgement. However, we're not the type to hold grudges or get sucked into the hype of 'he said, she said'. We're better than that, right?

Having said all that, we are more guilty than we care to admit, of getting caught up in the pressure of what everyone else thinks or expects. That being, society. We tend to fall into the trap without even knowing it, often expressed through phrases such as 'Oh my god I'm 30 and single', 'I'm 25 and I don't have a career yet, 'I really should buy a house already', 'All my friends are married and I'm not. I might as well call myself Bridget Jones' or 'I've really got to sort my shit out'. Think about it. If you've not said it or thought it, then there's a high probably another millennial you've had a conversation with, has. The pressure we place on ourselves—most often by osmosis from society—is immense and would in fact be quite humorous if those of us suffering took the odd chill pill and sat back and breathed every so often. But it's nothing to be shy about. We're all living in the same world of messages, suggestions, ideals, notions and exceptions and it's hard not to feel like we're caught up in the general vibes of pressure.

But to bring a little perspective: **no one is forcing your hand**.

It's time to listen up.

#Wake up

To start, we need to get real with ourselves. Yes, that's correct. The reality is we harbour values, qualities and beliefs that are different from other generations— something we need to get clear on, something we need to own. Sure, being in a world where we're more attuned to feeling like we're being moulded into a one-size-fits-all model or bent and squeezed into shape that would make even Gumby feel uncomfortable, it might feel hard to accept. Trust your own judgment and own your differences with a bit of millennial pizzaz.

#Quit playing games with my heart (thank you, Backstreet Boys)

Let's be honest. We know when we aren't being true or honest with ourselves. Our heart, gut and feelings are key indicators of whether something sits well with us. We know intuitively when something doesn't feel right. Often manifesting in the weight-in-the-pit-of-my-stomach feeling accompanied by increased bathroom habits. But, in recognising the reality that time is of the essence and we're already busting our chops trying to get shit done, it often doesn't leave much time for tapping into the self. That being, taking a moment to contemplate how we feel, while we let out the huge breath of air, we didn't realise we'd been holding on to. Now this of course must change—particularly if we want to avoid living someone else's makeshift dreams, rather than our own.

Our intuition provides a fail proof warning system—we just need to take the time to listen. Be your own Superhero; back yourself, be confident and start trusting what you feel, rather than worrying about what others think, or want. Detach from the 'shoulds', own who you are, and what you want. And, should the need arise, do stand up and give the finger to the rest of the world. Literally.

#Be a commitment-phobe and own it

No one likes to be the spoil sport of a party, or the player who consistently fails to show up for game day. But the truth is, we're a generation who place value in freedom. Freedom to choose what we do, who we do it with, and when. So why then do we feel the need to pigeonhole ourselves and make decisions about things we don't necessarily want right now? Or get our knickers in a twist, bitch and moan about the inability to have the things that society are forcing us to have, when we haven't even decided about whether we want it?

Take the home ownership versus renting debate. Renting gives us freedom. It's one less commitment (i.e. mortgage), one less stress (i.e. debt) and allows us to put money we can save into experiences—things we value (i.e. travel, good food, wellbeing). And to be honest, who wants to buy at a time of economic insecurity? The property market has dropped in Australia, with banks no longer lending to developers. Rising interest rates and tax reform have weighed on housing demand in the U.S., slowing growth. And with Brexit developments in the U.K., who knows the consequences and impacts to the housing market—not just in the U.K., but across Europe?

Yes, times are uncertain, but let's ride the wave. Things may in fact, turn in our favour. In the meantime, adopt your Mr Burns persona: mutter slowly in a low, sinister voice the word 'Excellent' while steepling your fingertips and patiently wait. Watch this space.

#Yes, money doesn't grow on trees, but we're not that hard done by

We've all heard the myths (yawn) around millennials and money. That none of us have savings, we are financially illiterate and spend all our money on smashed avocado toast rather than paying off our debt or saving for a mortgage. Well, studies are starting to provide some refreshing credibility to counter these ongoing misconceptions.[56] In fact, when it comes to money, we are a generation who wants bang for their buck—likely to show up in the form of shopping around, thinking about

---

[56] Macsmith, M., and McGllick, T. .2019. *The Australian Millennial Report 2019*. Millennial Future.

our purchases, bargain hunting and negotiating on price. Which is why we do have savings and can save money — in some cases, better than others.[57] And while we are living our lives more in the present moment and not so caught up in the future, we haven't written off buying homes or investing. It's more a case of it will happen when we're ready.

#Look around your own backyard

Let's be honest. At some point in time we've all wanted more than we have. A better job, more money, a bigger home, nicer car, more friends. A better life in fact. While there's no harm in wondering what a Kardashian life might be like, there is harm in measuring our life against someone else's. Yes, judgment is rife across society. We hear terms like 'recognition', 'status' and 'success' all the time. But it's these words that cause us to judge ourselves and judge others. When we start comparing our life to someone else's, we embark on a slippery slope of 'permission to criticise' ourselves, followed by the high probability that we will feel very ordinary about

---

[57] Ibid. While millennials are most concerned about the cost of living, economy and housing affordability, we can still save AU$235 per week, compared with AU$182 for the average Australian.

ourselves. Which, I might add, make us fools, because we do this to ourselves by choice. The fact is, we, regardless of the challenges we face, have everything we need to live a rewarding, fulfilling and meaningful life. And we all know what happens when we go sniffing around in someone else's backyard or territory or embark on an extra-marital affair. We come back with our tail between our legs, red faced and embarrassed. Point to note: The grass isn't greener on the other side. The grass is greener now, if we take the time to water it.

#Life is a game. Have fun with it

While none of us are immune to the influence others or society have on us, we do have the ability to be able to minimise the impacts on our lives. All the expectations and pressures we face from the world around us, are designed to test us. Think of it like a game: albeit you're on the field with nine billion other people. All these people around us, testing our strength in remaining true to ourselves and living the life we want. But equally, all of who, are simply doing their best, like us. It's these people we must thank for testing our own sense of self, our sense of worth and our resilience in remaining true to who we are. Living a life for us—rather than a life where we feel obligated to live by choices someone else or society have made.

***

Like the similarities that exist amongst us, it's the challenges that we face that equally make us unique. The times we are in, are for us. Challenges aside, when we take the time to contemplate where we are right now and what's on offer, it might not be the Rolls-Royce of conditions, but we are ok. Sure, it's not quite like we're living each day conquering Everest, but where we are at this point in time, is something to be proud of.

We are here to enjoy life, not be slaves to it. Be, do and have anything you want. When in doubt, flip the coin to Mr Brightside.[58]Come out of your cage, open your eager eyes, own who you are and what you want in life. The world is your oyster and will always remain that way. Be proudly you. Be proudly millennial.

#Power to millennials

---

[58] *Mr. Brightside* is a single realised by American rock band, The Killers.

Lightning Source UK Ltd.
Milton Keynes UK
UKHW021525250719
346803UK00005B/488/P